DEAD MOUNTAIN

THE **UNTOLD TRUE STORY** OF
THE DYATLOV PASS INCIDENT

DONNIE EICHAR

with
J.C. GABEL
and **NOVA JACOBS**

CHRONICLE BOOKS
SAN FRANCISCO

Library of Congress Cataloging-in-Publication Data
Eichar, Donnie, author.
  Dead Mountain: the untold true story of the Dyatlov Pass incident / by
Donnie Eichar.
     pages cm
  ISBN 978-1-4521-1274-9
  1. Hiking — Russia (Federation) — Ural Mountains Region. 2. Eichar,
Donnie — Travel — Russia (Federation) — Ural Mountains Region. 3. Moun-
taineering accidents — Russia (Federation) — Ural Mountains Region — 20th
century. 4. Ural Mountains Region (Russia) — History — 20th century. I.
Title.
  GV199.44.R82U734 2013
  914.743 — dc23
                       2013014843

Poem and song translations by Eugene Alper. "Snow" copyright © 1958
Aleksandr Gorodnitsky, translation presented by permission.

Manufactured in the United States.

Designed by EMILY DUBIN
Map by TIM TOMKINSON
Typeset by HOWIE SEVERSON

10 9 8 7 6 5 4 3 2 1

Chronicle Books LLC
680 Second Street
San Francisco, California 94107
www.chroniclebooks.com

To my son Dashiel,
never stop wondering.
And to my beautiful Julia,
without you it would not be.
I love you.
— D.E.

Igor Dyatlov, 1936-1959

Yuri Doroshenko,
1938–1959

Zinaida (Zina) Kolmogorova,
1937–1959

Alexander Kolevatov,
1934–1959

Alexander (Sasha) Zolotaryov,
1921–1959

Lyudmila (Lyuda) Dubinina,
1938–1959

Rustem (Rustik) Slobodin,
1936–1959

Yuri (Georgy) Krivonishchenko,
1934–1959

Nikolay (Kolya) Thibault-Brignoles,
1935–1959

Yuri Yudin,
1937–2013

Holatchahl mountain (a.k.a. Dead Mountain), 1959.
The location of the Dyatlov tent is in the
middle right of the frame.

CONTENTS

"*If I could ask God just one question it would be what really happened to my friends that night?*"

—YURI YUDIN

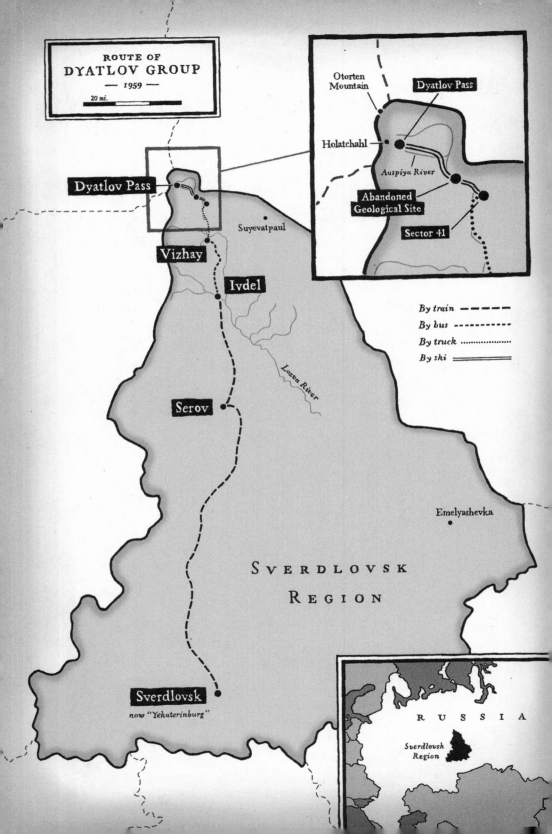

ROUTE OF
DYATLOV GROUP
— 1959 —
20 mi.

Dyatlov Pass

Otorten Mountain

Dyatlov Pass

Holatchahl

Auspiya River

Abandoned Geological Site

Sector 41

By train
By bus
By truck
By ski

Suyevatpaul

Vizhay

Ivdel

Lozva River

Serov

Emelyashevka

SVERDLOVSK

REGION

Sverdlovsk
now "Yekaterinburg"

RUSSIA

Sverdlovsk Region

AUTHOR'S NOTE

The following account is based on years of research into the case of the Dyatlov hikers. All facts are derived from the criminal case files in the Soviet archives, the hikers' own journals and photographs, and interviews conducted in Russia with the hikers' friends and family, as well as with those involved in the search efforts. This has been supported by interviews with scientists and various experts on the case. This book would not have been possible without the invaluable assistance of Vladimir Borzenkov, Yuri Kuntsevich and Yuri Yudin. When we set out to retrace the Dyatlov group's final steps in the winter of 2012, we had one goal: to piece together the truth of this half-century-old Russian mystery.

★

Prologue

TWO FIGURES TRUDGE ACROSS A SNOWY EXPANSE. THE peak of Otorten Mountain stands icy and grim in the distance, a lone witness to their miserable progress. It is afternoon, though difficult to say how late. Time of day tends to lose its meaning in this wilderness, where the sun is a mere smudge behind cloud cover, and the haze is so pervasive as to make earth and sky indistinguishable. The pair push forward into the headwind, their bundled bodies a fleck of punctuation on this vast, wintry page.

The men are university students in search of friends who have been missing ten days. They tell themselves that this is a rescue mission, not a recovery. After all, the nine missing hikers—seven men, two women—are highly accomplished, having completed numerous mountaineering expeditions into this region. In fact, the missing are members of the most esteemed hiking group at their school, and there is no reason to believe that they are not alive, counting the days until rescue. Perhaps the two men imagine a reunion of schoolmates just ahead, beyond the next snowdrift. . . . But, other than the occasional dwarf pine, there is nothing to see.

The sun is dropping. The searchers don't have much time before they must turn around and rejoin the rest of the team at base camp. Weather conditions are volatile in the northern Urals—snow can fly in fast and thick without warning, and hurricane-force winds are a persistent menace. Though the morning had given them clear skies, threatening clouds have since collected, and the wind is already whipping snow from the ground in prelude to a storm. It looks as if it may be another day lost. But then, through the disorienting blur, the men spy something that is neither rock nor tree—a dark, gray shape. As they draw closer, they find a flapping tent. Though its twin poles stand obediently in the wind, a section of the tarpaulin has surrendered under the weight of recent snows.

Conflicting thoughts of relief and horror flood the searchers' minds as they approach. They shout for their friends, but there is no reply. They pass an ice ax sticking out of the snow. Then a half-buried flashlight left in the on position, its battery spent. One of the men moves toward the partially snowbound entrance. The tent is a thick, canvas fortress, outfitted with a triple barrier of fabric and fasteners designed to keep out wind and cold. As the young man begins to clear away the snow, his companion looks for a faster way inside. He picks up the ice ax and, in several swift motions, brings it down on the canvas, fashioning his own entrance.

The men enter the buckled tent, their eyes immediately darting over its contents. As is typical of camping in this climate, an insulating layer of empty backpacks, padded coats and blankets lines the floor and periphery. At the south end of the tent's roughly 80 square feet are several pairs of ski boots. Six more pairs sit along another wall. Near the entrance lie a wood ax and saw. Most everything else has been stowed away in packs, but a few personal objects are visible: a camera, a can of money, a diary. The men share a wave of relief as they realize there are no bodies. But there is something curious about the place, the way everything is arranged—the ski boots standing in disciplined formation, the bags of bread and cereal positioned sensibly in one corner. The stove is in the center of the tent, not yet assembled, and an open flask of cocoa sits frozen nearby as if waiting to be reheated. There is also a cloth napkin bearing neat slices of ham. The entire arrangement gives the distinct impression of someone having tidied very recently, and, if not for the collapsed tarpaulin, one might expect a lively band of campers to return at any moment, kindling bundled in their arms.

The men step back into the snow to consider their discovery. They give in to a moment of cautious celebration, comforted in the idea that their comrades have not perished, but are out there somewhere, perhaps in a snow cave. As the two scan the immediate landscape, not once does it cross their minds that a forsaken camp is cause for anything but hope. Yet they cannot begin to fathom the conditions that must have compelled their friends—all nine of them—to abandon their only shelter and vanish into the stark cruelty of the Russian wilderness.

★

1

2012

IT IS NEARLY TWENTY BELOW ZERO AS I CRUNCH THROUGH knee-deep snow in the direction of Dyatlov Pass. It's the middle of winter and I have been trekking with my Russian companions through the northern Ural Mountains for over eight hours and I'm anxious to reach our destination, but it's becoming increasingly difficult to put one foot in front of the other. Visibility is low, and the horizon is lost in a milky-white veil of sky and ground. Only the occasional dwarf pine, pushing through the snow's crust, reminds me that there is dormant life beneath my feet. The knee-high boots I am wearing—an "Arctic Pro" model I purchased on the Internet two months ago—are supposed to be shielding my feet from the most glacial temperatures. Yet at the moment the inner toes of my right foot are frozen together, and I am already having dark visions of amputation. I don't complain, of course. The last time I expressed any hint of dissatisfaction, my guide Vladimir leaned over and said, "*This is Siberia.*" I later learn this isn't technically Siberia, only the gateway. The real Siberia, which stretches to the east all the way to the Pacific Ocean, begins on the other side of the Ural Mountains. But then "Siberia," historically, has been less a geographical designation than a state of mind, a looming threat—the frozen hell on earth to which czarist and Communist Russias sent their political undesirables. By this definition, Siberia is not so much a place as it is a hardship to endure, and perhaps that's what Vladimir means when he says that we are in Siberia. I trudge on.

I have taken two extended trips to Russia, traveled over 15,000 miles, left my infant son and his mother and drained all of my savings in order to be here. And now we are less than a mile away from our terminus: Holatchahl (sometimes transliterated as "Kholat-Syakhyl"), a name that means "Dead Mountain" in Mansi, the indigenous language of the region. The 1959 tragedy on Holatchahl's eastern slope has since become so famous that the area is officially referred to as Dyatlov Pass, in honor of the leader of the hiking group that perished there. This last leg of our journey will not be easy: The mountain is extremely remote, the cold punishing and my companions tell me I am the first American to attempt this route in wintertime. At the moment I don't find this distinction particularly inspiring or comforting. I force my attention away from my frozen toes and to our single objective: Find the location of the tent where nine hikers met their end over half a century ago.

Just over two years ago I would never have imagined myself here. Two years ago I had never heard the name *Dyatlov* or the incident synonymous with it. I stumbled upon the case quite by accident, while doing research for a scripted film project I was developing in Idaho—one that had nothing to do with hikers or Russia. My interest in the half-century-old mystery started out innocently enough, at a level one might have for a particularly compelling Web site to which one returns compulsively. In fact, I did scour the Internet for every stray detail, quickly exhausting all the obvious online sources, both reliable and sketchy. My attraction to the Dyatlov case turned fanatical and all-consuming, and I became desperate for more information.

The bare facts were these: In the early winter months of 1959, a group of students and recent graduates from the Ural Polytechnic Institute (now Ural State Technical University) departed from the city of Sverdlovsk (as Yekaterinburg was known during the Soviet era) on an expedition to Otorten Mountain in the northern Urals.

All members of the group were experienced in lengthy ski tours and mountain expeditions, but, given the time of year, their route was estimated to be of the highest difficulty—a designation of Grade III. Ten days into the trip, on the first of February, the hikers set up camp for the night on the eastern slope of Holatchahl mountain. That evening, an unknown incident sent the hikers fleeing from their tent into the darkness and piercing cold. Nearly three weeks later, after the group failed to return home, government authorities dispatched a search and rescue team. The team discovered the tent, but found no initial sign of the hikers. Their bodies were eventually found roughly a mile away from their campsite, in separate locations, half-dressed in subzero temperatures. Some were found facedown in the snow; others in fetal position; and some in a ravine clutching one another. Nearly all were without their shoes.

After the bodies were transported back to civilization, the forensic analysis proved baffling. While six of the nine had perished of hypothermia, the remaining three had died from brutal injuries, including a skull fracture. According to the case files, one of the victims was missing her tongue. And when the victims' clothing was tested for contaminants, a radiologist determined certain articles to contain abnormal levels of radiation.

After the close of the investigation, the authorities barred access to Holatchahl mountain and the surrounding area for three years. The lead investigator, Lev Ivanov, wrote in his final report that the hikers had died as a result of "an unknown compelling force," a euphemism that, despite the best efforts of modern science and technological advances, still defines the case fifty-plus years later.

With no eyewitnesses and over a half century of extensive yet inconclusive investigations, the Dyatlov hiking tragedy continues to elude explanation. Numerous books have been published in Russia on the subject, varying in quality and level of research, and with most of the authors refuting the others' claims. I was surprised to learn that none of these Russian authors had ever been to the site of the tragedy in the winter. Speculation in these books and elsewhere ranged from the mundane to the crackpot: avalanche, windstorm, murder, radiation exposure, escaped-prisoner attack, death by shock wave or explosion, death by nuclear waste, UFOs, aliens, a vicious bear attack and a freak winter tornado. There is even a theory that the hikers drank a potent moonshine, resulting in their instant blindness. In the last two decades, some authors have suggested that the hikers had witnessed a top-secret missile launch—a periodic occurrence in the Urals at the height of the Cold War—and had been killed for it. Even self-proclaimed skeptics, who attempt to cut through the intrigue in order to posit scientific explanations, are spun into a web of conspiracy theories and disinformation.

One heartbreaking fact, however, remained clear to me: Nine young people died under inexplicable circumstances, and many of their family members have since passed away without ever knowing what happened to their loved ones. Would the remaining survivors go to their graves with the same unanswered questions?

In my work as a documentary filmmaker, my job has been to uncover the facts of a story and piece them together in a compelling fashion for an audience. Whatever external events might draw me to a story, I am interested in people with consuming passions. And in examining the fates of passionate characters, I am often pulled back in time to explore the history behind their personal victories and tragedies. Whether I was stepping into the psyche of the first blind Ironman triathletes in *Victory Over Darkness*, or untangling the fate of late photojournalist Dan Eldon for my short documentary *Dan Eldon Lives Forever*, I was ultimately looking to solve a human puzzle.

I had certainly found a puzzle in the Dyatlov incident, but my fascination with the case went beyond a desire to find a solution. The Dyatlov hikers, when not in school, had been exploring loosely charted territory in an age before Internet and GPS. The setting—the Soviet Union at the height of the Cold War—could not have been further from that of my own upbringing, but there was a purity to the hikers' travels that resonated with me.

I grew up in the 1970s and '80s on the central Gulf Coast of Florida, the land of limitless sunshine. I had been born to teen-age parents and there was a free, easygoing quality to my entire childhood. When I wasn't in school, you could find me fishing or surfing in the warm coastal waters. In the summer of 1987, when I was fifteen, I took a trip with my father to the surfers' playground of Costa Rica. It was my first trip out of the country, and at a time when tourists were not yet flocking to Central America. The resources available to off-the-grid travelers were limited, and my dad and I had to rely on mail-order maps to direct us to the country's best surf beaches. When the maps arrived, I'd spread them out on the kitchen table and study the curves of the coastline and the comically specific instructions that hinted at adventure: "Pay off the locals with *colones* to access this gate" or "look for huge tree near river mouth to find wave."

As soon as we stepped off the plane in San José, with only our maps and a single Spanish phrase book to guide us, we were weightless, living moment to moment. In the following days, we rode flawless waves on secluded beaches, camped out under tranquil moonlight, survived insect infestations, and shared our space with howler monkeys, crocodiles and boa constrictors. Our far-flung adventures created a sense of camaraderie and shared heroism between my dad and me. Though I would hardly compare tropical Central America with subarctic Russia, memories of that time lent to my appreciation of why these young Soviets had repeatedly risked the dangers of the Ural wilderness in exchange for the fellowship that outdoor travel brings.

There was, of course, the central mystery of the case, with its bewildering set of clues. Why would nine experienced outdoorsmen and -women rush out of their tent, insufficiently clothed, in twenty-five-degrees-below-zero conditions and walk a mile toward certain death? One or two of them might have made the unfathomable mistake of leaving the safety of camp, but all nine? I could find no other case in which the bodies of missing hikers were found, and yet after a criminal investigation and forensic examinations, there was no explanation given for the events leading to their deaths. And while there are cases throughout history of single hikers or mountaineering groups disappearing without a trace, in those instances, the cause of death is quite clear—either they had encountered an avalanche or had fallen into a crevasse. I wondered how, in our globalized world of instant access to an unprecedented amount of data, and our sophisticated means of pooling our efforts, a case like this could remain so stubbornly unsolved.

My investigative synapses really started to fire when I learned that the single surviving member of the Dyatlov group, Yuri Yudin, was still alive. Yudin had been the tenth member of the hiking group, until he decided to turn back early from the expedition. Though he couldn't have known it at the time, it was a decision that would save his life. It must also, I imagined, have left him with a chronic case of survivor's guilt. I calculated that Yudin would now be in his early to mid-seventies. And though he rarely talked to the press, I wondered: Could he be persuaded to come out of his seclusion?

Although my initial efforts to find Yudin got me nowhere, I was able to make contact with Yuri Kuntsevich, the head of the Dyatlov Foundation in Yekaterinburg, Russia. Kuntsevich explained that the foundation's mission was both to preserve the memories of the hikers and to uncover the truth of the 1959 tragedy. According to Kuntsevich, not all the files from the Dyatlov case had been made public, and the foundation was hoping to persuade Russian officials to reopen the criminal investigation. Speaking through a translator, he was perfectly cordial and offered that he might have information to help my understanding of the incident. However, my specific queries about the case—including how to reach Yuri Yudin—resulted in only vague or cryptic responses. At last he put the onus on me: "If you seek the truth in this case, you must come to Russia."

Kuntsevich had no real idea who I was—I had introduced myself as a filmmaker and we'd spoken for forty-five minutes—yet he had extended an unambiguous invitation. Or was it a summons? I was not Russian. I didn't speak the language. I had seen snow less than a dozen times in my life. Who was I to go roaming through Russia in the middle of winter to unravel one of the country's most baffling mysteries?

As I approached Dyatlov Pass more than two years later, pausing every so often to blow warm air into my gloves, I found myself asking the same question: Why am I here?

Igor Dyatlov, ca. 1957-1958

★

2

Рюкзаков, по традиции, легких,
Погоды—хорошей всегда,
Зимой—не слишком морозной,
А летом—чтоб не жара.

Let your backpacks be light,
weather always fine,
winter not too cold,
and summer without heat.

—Georgy Krivonishchenko, excerpt from New Year's poem, 1959

IF ONE HAD BEEN ABLE TO GLIMPSE INSIDE DORMITORY 531 on January 23, 1959, one would have seen the very picture of fellowship, youth, and happiness. The room itself was nothing to look at. Like most dorms at Sverdlovsk's Ural Polytechnic Institute, the furnishings were serviceable at best; and, for half the year, the building rumbled under the toil of a coal-stoked boiler. One might have assumed in observing the room—with its blistered wallpaper, lumpy mattresses and lingering odors from the communal kitchen—that the students residing here must take pleasure in things outside material comforts. They must certainly

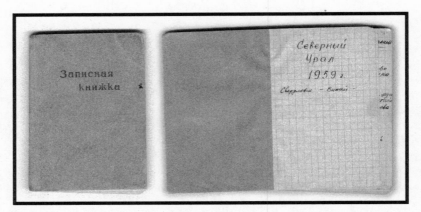

The front cover and first page of the Dyatlov group's diary.

live for books, art, friends and nature, interests that could carry them beyond this dingy cupboard. And one would be right. On that fourth Friday in January, a month before the school term was to begin, nine friends in their early twenties were engaged in last-minute preparations for a trip that would take them far beyond the confines of dormitory life.

The room that evening was charged with excitement, each member of the group busy with a designated task and each talking over the others in an eagerness to be heard. Their group diary captured snatches of their conversation:

We've forgotten salt!
Igor! Where are you?
Where's Doroshenko, why doesn't he take 20 packages?
Will we play mandolin on the train?
Where are the scales?
Damn, it does not fit in!
Who has the knife?

One of the young men stuffed food into a backpack, trying to find the most space-efficient configuration for multiple bags of oats and cans of meat. Nearby, his friend catalogued medicines. Another searched desperately for mislaid footwear.

Where are my leather boots?

The group's twenty-three-year-old leader, Igor Dyatlov, was overseeing these final preparations with somber concentration. Igor was lean and strong, with a head of closely cropped hair. His mouth was almost feminine, and his eyes wide set. He wasn't classically handsome, yet there was something arresting about his face, something expressive that spoke of a rich interior life and strong self-possession. He was famous at the school's hiking club for his technical know-how and the easy command he took over any situation. "Igor had indisputable authority," remembered his friend and hiking mentor Volodya Poloyanov years later. "Everyone wanted to go on a trip under his leadership, but one had to earn the honor to get in Igor's group."

Igor had been born into a family of engineers and at an early age had shown a finely tuned, scientific mind. He was studying radio engineering at UPI, and despite the official Soviet ban on shortwave radio transmissions during the Cold War, his bedroom at home was outfitted with radio panels, homemade receivers, and a shortwave radio. "Thanks to Igor, we had a handmade radio receiver on our hiking trips," Poloyanov said. "His technical knowledge was encyclopedic." Another hiking friend, Moisey Akselrod, recalled of a 1958 trip to the Sayan Mountains in southern Siberia, "Dyatlov's major contribution was his amazing ultrashortwave transmitters that were used for communications between rafts."

Despite Igor's affection for wireless devices, he would not be packing a radio for this particular trip. Shortwave radios of the time were cumbersome, and hauling them into the Russian wilderness in winter would have been out of the question. Besides, Igor had his hands full ensuring his group packed the essentials. If they were to forget something, there would be no stopping for extra supplies in the middle of the Ural Mountains, and no one wanted to be responsible for neglecting to pack something potentially lifesaving. This was a pivotal trip for Igor and his friends. They were all Grade II hikers, but if this particular excursion went as planned, the group would be awarded Grade III certification upon their return. It was the highest hiking certification in the country at the time, one that required candidates to cover at least 186 miles (300 kilometers) of ground, with a third of those miles in challenging terrain. The minimum duration of the trip was to be sixteen days, with no fewer than eight of those spent in uninhabited regions, and at least six nights spent in a tent. If the hikers met these conditions, their new certification would allow them to teach others their craft as Masters of Sport. It was a distinction that Igor and his group badly wanted.

Nearby, scribbling in her diary, sat one of the two women in the room—Zinaida Kolmogorova. Like Igor, she was a student of radio engineering, though the subject didn't come as naturally to her as it did him. To her friends, "Zina" was regarded as lively and bright, always ready with an amusing remark or engaging story. But at that moment the pretty tomboy was silent. Having been appointed the diarist for that evening, she felt obliged to record the last moments of preparation for the collective records. Her finely sculpted face and large, brown eyes were tilted toward the page, intent on capturing the mood of departure. How to describe the room? *The room is in artistic disorder.* . . . Zina was the type of girl who drew admiration wherever she went. In fact, several of her companions had secret crushes on her.

Lyudmila Dubinina, or "Lyuda," was the other woman in the room and at twenty years old, the youngest of the group. She was a student of construction-industry economics and was a serious

Lyudmila "Lyuda" Dubinina taken
during a summer hiking tour, n.d.

A previous group hiking tour with Zinaida "Zina" Kolmogorova
(fourth from right with round white sunglasses), n.d.

person, a quality evident in her assigned duty that evening: counting the money and rolling it tightly into a waterproof can. Lyuda
was strong, and capable of enduring intense pain and discomfort.
On a previous hiking trip, she had been shot in the leg after a companion mishandled a hunting rifle. Though she had to be carried

out of Siberia's Eastern Sayan Mountains over 50 miles of rugged terrain, she kept her companions in good spirits the entire journey.

In addition to Lyuda's reputation as an outspoken and highly principled student, she was a fervent communist. Had she been wearing a uniform, one might have imagined she'd stepped off a Communist propaganda poster. In fact, there was a name in the USSR for such young women—"the girl in a red kerchief with a gun."

On that evening, Yuri Yudin—one of three Yuris in the group—busied himself with packing the medicine kit. With his boyish face and a set of pronounced teeth that erupted from his mouth whenever he smiled, the geology student was the image of ease and good humor. Having suffered lifelong problems with rheumatism, a heart condition, and chronic knee and back pain, Yudin was also the least likely member of the group. He had previously been forced to take a year off from school due to an illness, but hiking had restored his vitality. Given his recurring struggles with his health, his role as the keeper of the medicine was certainly fitting.

Besides Igor, Zina, Lyuda and Yudin, there were five others: Yuri Doroshenko—"Doroshenko"—studied radio engineering at UPI with Zina and Igor. He was impulsive and brave, and carried an aura of myth about him, maybe because of the time he chased off a bear on a camping trip with nothing more than his nerve and a geologist's hammer.

Yuri Krivonishchenko—"Georgy"—was the group's resident jester and musician, always ready with wisecracks and a mandolin. He had a big personality and a talent for storytelling, prompting one friend to dub him "Zina with pants." When Georgy wasn't singing or pulling pranks, he was a student of construction and hydraulics.

Alexander Kolevatov—"Kolevatov"—was a methodical young man with an imposing physical presence. In his downtime from studying nuclear physics, he loved to puff on his antique pipe. He was also an intensely private person and often reluctant to share his journal entries with his comrades.

Yuri Doroshenko (top row, far right), Zinaida "Zina" Kolmogorova
(second row, far right), and Yuri Blinov (bottom row, center), next
to Igor Dyatlov, in striped cap, on a hiking tour, May 1, 1957.

Rustem Slobodin—"Rustik"—could be called the group's rich
kid. He was the son of affluent university professors, and had
already earned a degree in mechanical engineering. Like Georgy,
he was musically gifted and enjoyed playing mandolin. Though
one might have expected him to possess an elitist air, Rustik was
as unpretentious and friendly as they come.

And, lastly, there was Nikolay Thibault-Brignoles—"Kolya"—
distinguished by his foreign name and background. He was the
great-grandson of a Frenchman who had immigrated to Russia in
the 1880s to work in the Ural factories. Kolya had already earned his
degree, in industrial civil construction. Though serious and exceedingly well read, he always looked for the humor in any situation.

These seven men and two women, stooped under the weight
of their packs and in a nervous bundle of excitement, left room
531 and descended the four flights of stairs. After piling out of the
building and into the sharp January chill, they headed for the tram

that would take them to the train station a few miles from campus. Twenty minutes later, when the tram arrived at the station, the friends realized they were cutting it close to the train's departure. As the group made an awkward dash for the entrance, there was no time for final departing glances over their dark, sooty town.

The nine companions found their way to their *platzkart*, or third-class compartment. Employing a popular scheme of Russian students traveling on a budget, the group had deliberately purchased fewer tickets than they needed. In the event that the conductor passed through their car to punch tickets, a couple of the hikers would hide under their wooden seats. Lyuda was particularly adept at this maneuver, and over the course of the trip, she would take advantage of her compact size to evade the conductor's watchful eye.

As the group settled in, they noticed that their numbers had suddenly increased by one. There was a newcomer in their midst— an acquaintance of Igor's who had asked to tag along at the last minute. As eight pairs of eyes settled on and assessed Alexander Zolotaryov, it was apparent to everyone that he was old. Well, *older*—thirty-seven, to be exact. Igor introduced him to the others, explaining that Zolotaryov was a local hiking instructor and a valuable addition to the team. Zolotaryov had originally intended to set off with student hiker Sergey Sogrin and his group, who were headed further north into the subpolar Urals, but when Sogrin's timetable didn't suit Zolotaryov, Sogrin introduced him to Igor. The timing was perfect, as another hiker, Nikolay Popov, had recently dropped out of Igor's party.

"Just call me Sasha," the newcomer told them with a flash of gold teeth. Besides having a mouth full of metal, Sasha also had several tattoos. The name Gena had been inked on the back of his right hand, and when he pushed up his sleeves, a picture of beets could be glimpsed on his right forearm. Tattoos were relatively unusual for the average Russian citizen in 1959, but they were common among veterans. Sasha had, in fact, seen combat in World War II.

After the initial surprise of finding a stranger among them subsided, the friends relaxed into their seats and chatted with the hiking groups around them. Igor and the others were happy to discover that one of their hiking-club friends, Yuri Blinov, was seated in their train car. Blinov's party was taking the same route north to Ivdel, and the two groups would be able to keep each other company over the coming days.

The Dyatlov group's departure may not have gone as smoothly as they'd hoped, but as the train pulled out of the station, the friends' very best selves emerged. It wasn't long before they embraced the company of the outsider. And when Georgy produced his mandolin, and Sasha began to sing, it was as if he had been one of them all along. The ten friends sang for hours. The group's favorite was "The Globe," a song about the joys of travel.

Our voices will carry on
Over mountain ridges and peaks,
Over February blizzards and storms,
Over vast expanses of snow.

We will hear each other's song
Though hundreds of miles lie between us,
Though far from each other we roam,
Friends' singing will beat the distance.

Hours later, after they had sung through and committed their new melodies to memory, Zina pulled out her diary and scribbled her final thoughts for the day.

I wonder what awaits us in this hike? Will anything new happen? Oh yes, the boys have given a solemn oath not to smoke through the whole trip. I wonder how strong their willpower is, will they manage without cigarettes? We are going to sleep, and Ural woods loom behind the windows.

Ural Polytechnic Institute, 1959.

Igor Dyatlov, at far left, in class, n.d.

★

3

ON THE EASTERN SIDE OF THE URAL MOUNTAINS, 1,036 miles from Moscow, lies Yekaterinburg, Russia's fourth largest city and home of the Ural Polytechnic Institute. It is a gray, industrial settlement positioned at the edge of fertile wetlands; beyond it looms the startling and seemingly endless beauty of the mountains. The city's population of 779,000 is surrounded on all sides by a thick blanket of evergreen, interrupted by pockets of swampland, ink-black lakes and quiet villages. It is a pristine setting for such a hardened town—one known for its machine and military hardware factories—and the contrast between the surrounding natural beauty and the city's industrial grime is striking. Yekaterinburg enjoys balmy weather for half of the year, but the other half finds its streets blanketed in discolored snow and its skies darkened with cumulus gusts of factory smoke. At least, this is how the city could be characterized in 1959, when it was known by its Soviet name, Sverdlovsk.

As part of the Soviets' drastic renunciation of monarchic rule— and, by association, the country's Westernization by Peter the Great two centuries earlier—cities such as Yekaterinburg had undergone a kind of rechristening, if an atheistic one. In the mid-1920s, it seemed that every city was getting a new name—most famously, Petrograd (formerly St. Petersburg) became Leningrad, and the city of Volgograd became Stalingrad. But all the name-changing in

Russia couldn't chase Peter the Great's heritage from the country or from Yekaterinburg—a city named for the ruler's wife, Catherine. Peter's architectural influence can still be seen in the city's neoclassical buildings and in the intense pride its inhabitants take in their educational institutions. Perhaps the finest of these is the Ural State Technical University, known for much of its life as the Ural Polytechnic Institute, or UPI.

In 1959, UPI—along with many of the educational institutions in the Soviet Union—was experiencing a kind of renaissance. Khrushchev had taken office a few years earlier with aims to alleviate the cultural suppression of the Stalin years. His reforms resulted in a rapid flowering of the arts, sciences and athletics—a nationwide post-Stalinist softening known as "the Thaw." For artists and intellectuals, the Khrushchev years were badly needed irrigation after decades of cultural drought.

"Few men in history have had such long and devastating effects—and not only on their own countries but on the whole world as a whole—[as Stalin]," writes Robert Conquest in the introduction to his definitive study of the Russian leader, *Stalin: Breaker of Nations*. "For two whole generations Stalin's heritage has lain heavy on the chests.of a dozen nations, and the threat of it has loomed over all the others, in the fearful possibility of nuclear war. Stalin, to whom the aura of death clings so strongly, is himself only now ceasing to live on in the system he created. When he died in 1953 he left a monster whose own death throes are not yet over, more than a generation later."

Even so, after Stalin's death, intellectual society opened up for the first time since the Bolshevik Revolution, resulting in more freedoms and opportunities for everyday people. This heady and short-lived period in Russian history was particularly liberating for those who had survived the devastating losses of World War II and, before that, the punishing show trials of the '30s—famously

40

fictionalized in Arthur Koestler's novel *Darkness at Noon*—during which Stalin had imprisoned and murdered perceived political rivals.

In the mid- to late-'50s, for the first time in decades, young Russians felt a renewed sense of promise—sports, the arts, technology and accessible education were all part of this new optimism. It was a hopeful period that wouldn't recur in Russian history until the fall of the Soviet Union some three decades later. By Soviet standards, the Thaw was an exhilarating time to be young, physically fit and intellectually curious. The ten members of the Dyatlov group were all of these.

IT IS IN THIS YEAR OF CULTURAL FLOWERING, 1959, ON a day in February, that Igor Dyatlov's younger sister, Rufina, is leaving campus. At twenty-one years old, she is a pretty version of her brother, with a penetrating gaze and the well-defined bone structure found often in Slavic faces. The siblings are close and share a passion for science and technology. Rufina is, in fact, following Igor's example by majoring in radio engineering at UPI.

Mid-February is the time of year when campus fills up with students recently returned from home or—in the case of the sports club—hiking expeditions. By now most of the hiking groups have returned in time for the new term, their young minds and lungs invigorated by the recent weeks spent in crisp mountain air. But Rufina's brother is not among the returned. In fact, Rufina has just come from a frustrating meeting at the administrative building. It is February 16, three days after Igor was due home, and no one seems particularly worried.

Perhaps the university's lack of concern is due to the hiking commission's having thoroughly checked the soundness of Igor's proposed route. Or maybe it's because delays are routine in the world of mountaineering, particularly in winter. With no way for the hikers to communicate with their hometown—aside from the occasional telegram sent from an outpost—should they run up against delays, there is little for their families to do but wait.

Rufina is not looking forward to informing her family that her errand at the university has failed. Perhaps she will keep the news from her twelve-year-old sister, Tatiana, who is still so young and very attached to her older brother. Tatiana needn't know that the school administrators were unsympathetic to Rufina's pleas, and that they had given her only noncommittal responses and baseless assurances. A group of student hikers is missing, Rufina thinks, and no one outside the hikers' families seems to care. Not that she didn't detect a degree of unease among the members of the UPI sports club, but most everyone seems to agree that Igor, their hiking star, and his companions are simply late. Delays happen. All it takes is one hiker to sprain an ankle and the progress of the entire group slows to a hobble.

But Rufina knows her brother and is familiar with his strengths as an outdoorsman. Igor, in the fashion of their older brother, Slava, is a *tourist*—though not in the Western sense of the word. A *tourist* in the Russian sense is much closer to *adventurer*: a hiker or skier who journeys into the wilderness to explore new territory and push past personal limits of endurance. And Igor, in the eyes of his fellow hikers, is a *tourist* of the highest magnitude. But where his classmates at the hiking club see this as reason to expect his return, Rufina only finds more cause for worry. If a man as capable and careful as her brother hasn't returned by now, she reasons, it could only mean that something is very wrong.

Rufina thinks back to Igor's previous trips, searching for some kind of precedent for his absence. She thinks of his love of nature and how his strong visual talents informed his entire approach to nature. His deep love of the outdoors was evident in the way he wrote about his hiking trips in his journals.

Photo taken by Igor
Dyatlov, 1958.

July 8. We are in a beautiful meadow, walking along blossoming
willow-weed, chamomile, and bluebell. The grass is high, so we
walk in single file. The flat, expansive meadow is surrounded
by hills, and far away we can see the bluish foothills of the Ural
Mountains. The air is warm, the smell of grass is intoxicating,
and the birds are chirping—what a dream!

Most of the journal entries from Igor's trips read this way: tranquil, with a deep appreciation for the plant and animal life of the
Urals. There might have been trips during which her brother was
caught by surprise by some unforeseen danger, but there had been
nothing he wasn't capable of handling. There was that trip a couple
summers ago when Igor and his friends encountered a herd of wild
horses, an incident documented in the group's journal:

Suddenly from behind comes a powerful roar, of some unknown origin but approaching very quickly. We look back and freeze in terror: heading toward us is a herd of wild horses—many, many of them, a whole bunch! The first thought is run! But where to?! Igor commands firmly: "Stop! Nobody move!" We gather in a tight group, some covering their eyes, others with eyes wide open in horror, watching in complete silence the herd of about thirty horses racing towards us at full speed! About fifteen meters before they smash into us, the herd suddenly splits into two and, without slowing down, streams around us, like the river around a rock, and continues on its way.

But summer in the Ural Mountains presents an entirely different set of dangers from those of winter. Rufina knows that winter hiking is far more perilous than hiking in any other season, and that the sooner the university begins to look for her brother, the better her family's chances of bringing him home safe.

IGOR DYATLOV'S FAMILY IS NOT ALONE IN THEIR UNEASE. On February 13, the day of the Dyatlov group's appointed return, and in the days following, family members of the hikers begin to express their worry. The parents of Rustik Slobodin are the first to express outward concern. Rustik's father, Professor Vladimir Slobodin, who teaches at a local agricultural university, phones the UPI Sports Club, at which point he is informed that Lev Gordo, the middle-aged director of the club, is himself on a trip and won't be returning for several days. Until Gordo returns, the professor is told, little can be done.

As two more days pass, the university's telephones ring with repeated calls from nervous relatives. They are told variations of the same thing: The Dyatlov group is delayed, the president of the club is absent, nothing can be done at the moment, please be patient. But for the parents of the hikers, assurances from the sports club mean little in the conspicuous absence of their children, and they stay close to the phone. On February 17, bowing to pressure, university officials send an inquiring telegram to Vizhay, the village from which the Dyatlov group would be traveling. Meanwhile, the families make a request to the university for search planes. The request is refused.

The following day, club director Lev Gordo returns from his dacha to discover the tempest that has been brewing in his absence. But today, the university is in a position to give the families information, though not the information they are hoping for. A reply telegram has come from Vizhay: "The Dyatlov group did not return."

This turns out to be the necessary incitement for the university to take action, and a Colonel Georgy Ortyukov, a lecturer of reserve-officer training at UPI, takes charge of assembling a formal search party for the missing hikers. Lev Gordo, meanwhile, together with UPI student Yuri Blinov—whose group had shadowed Dyatlov's on the first leg of their trip—is assigned to travel the following day to Ivdel, the gateway to the northern Urals.

But the search party's efforts are stymied before they've begun: The Dyatlov group's approved route is nowhere to be found at the local hiking commission. Either the route has been lost or was never filed. Though their general destination north is known, there is no way to know precisely which route they took within those mountains. Without a definitive map of the hikers' course, the search party might as well be stepping into the Russian wilderness half blind.

On Friday, February 20, the search for the missing hikers officially begins. Gordo and Blinov fly out from Sverdlovsk by military helicopter and arrive later that day in Ivdel. From there, they take a Yak-12 surveillance plane north toward Vizhay, up the Lozva River, over an abandoned mine, and past Sector 41—a cluster of log cabins populated by woodcutters. The plane then veers west to the Severnaya Toshemka River, where the pair scan the Ural ridge and western Ural slopes. But before they can get far, clouds and strong winds force them to turn back to the airfield for the night.

On the same day Gordo and Blinov are scanning the northern Urals by air, UPI student Yuri Yudin has returned to Sverdlovsk for the new school term. Because he was assumed to be among Igor Dyatlov's group, his peers are surprised to see his face, and he is put in the position of explaining his peculiar non-absence. During the trip, Yudin's chronic back pain had reached incapacitating levels, forcing him to turn back early. But instead of returning directly to Sverdlovsk, Yudin had taken a detour to spend the rest of winter break in his home village of Emelyashevka, about 150 miles northeast of Sverdlovsk. There, he took his time and enjoyed the company of his family, unaware of what was happening back at school.

Now, upon his return to campus, Yudin is surprised to learn that his friends have not returned. He knows Igor and the rest were running three days behind, a fact Yudin now realizes he forgot to relay by telegram to the university. Now the original three days of delay has become six. But Yudin is not yet convinced this is cause for alarm, and on his first day back at school, he buries himself in his geology studies and puts his friends out of his mind. Perhaps he believes he is partly to blame for all the fuss. If he had only communicated the Dyatlov party's delay in the first place, he might have saved the university all this worry. It will be several days before Yudin begins to register his own alarm.

The next day Gordo and Blinov are in the air again, the weather has greatly improved since the previous day. They fly to the Vizhay riverhead and over the Anchucha tributary, which is the territory of the region's indigenous people: the Mansi. Along with a neighboring tribe, the Khanty, the Mansi occupy sections of the Urals and northwestern Siberia. Their numbers are small, around 6,400, and they live in villages whose economies revolve around hunting, fishing and the herding of reindeer.

The first search team boards a helicopter in Ivdel,
February 20, 1959.

Chopper drop-off for search and rescue, February 1959.

Upon landing, Gordo and Blinov approach the Mansi village of Bahtiyarova, a cluster of traditional yurts insulated with reindeer hides. There, the two men learn that a group of student hikers had stopped for tea in the village several weeks before. They were the guests of tribesman Pyotr Bahtiyarov, whose family gives the village its name. The hikers' stay was reportedly brief, and after they finished their tea, the group moved on, electing not to stay the night. After extracting what information they can from the Mansi, Blinov and Gordo take off again, flying west to the Urals. When they peer out the windows, they are able to make out the tracks of a Mansi sleigh below—evidently a native courtesy in seeing off departing guests. The tracks lead away from Bahtiyarov's yurt and heading west toward the Urals. But the tracks stop short of the tree line, and from there, any trace of the nine hikers seems to dissolve into the wild.

A diagram used by the rescue teams of the Vizhay forestry area indicating highways and local roads.

Graveyard monument to the Dyatlov group,
Mikhaylovskoye Cemetery, Yekaterinburg.

★

4

IN NOVEMBER 2010, THREE MONTHS AFTER MY INITIAL
phone call with Yuri Kuntsevich, and nine months after I'd learned
of the Dyatlov tragedy, I found myself traveling to Russia for the
first time. The timing wasn't ideal. My girlfriend, Julia, was seven
months pregnant and we were going through all the related joys
and upheaval of becoming parents. But we also knew that once
the baby arrived, there would be little time for me to spend on
the case—so to Russia I went. My close friend of twelve years and
film-producing partner, Jason Thompson, graciously agreed to
drop everything in order to join me on the trip. Jason shared my
enthusiasm for the Dyatlov case and my need to know what happened
to the hikers. We flew into Moscow and caught a connecting plane
east to Yekaterinburg by way of Aeroflot. Founded by the Soviet
government in 1923, Aeroflot is one of the oldest airlines in the world
and is the same state-owned airline whose planes were employed in
the search for the Dyatlov hikers. In fact, the company's original
insignia, a winged hammer-and-sickle that was emblazoned on
the sides of the rescue planes, is still used by the company today.

I was unsure what would happen once we touched down in
Yekaterinburg, but I had decided to tamp down the neurotic pro-
ducer side of my personality and just let the trip wash over me. At
this point, my dedication to the project was still in the exploratory
stage. I had been initially obsessed with the case, sure, but I wasn't

certain how much of my life I could realistically afford to devote to it. Even so, I kept turning over the same questions: What led the hikers to leave their only shelter? Could the explanation be as simple as an avalanche? Were there really still classified case files hidden away in the Russian archives, as Kuntsevich had told me on the phone? And where was Yuri Yudin?

Over my final weeks of trip preparation, I had also become eager to make contact with Igor Dyatlov's younger sisters, Tatiana and Rufina, who were rumored to still be living near Yekaterinburg. But like Yudin, after half a century of invasive questions from writers and journalists—many concerning unsubstantiated and salacious claims about the hikers' personal lives (a lover's quarrel, jealousy, group in-fighting)—they weren't exactly handing out interviews.

It was early morning when we landed just southeast of Yekaterinburg at the Koltsovo International Airport. Built under Stalin in the 1920s as a military air base, the airport was now an international hub, the fifth largest in the country. At that point, I was grateful to have Jason by my side to share my total disorientation and lack of anything resembling a plan. All I knew was that we were meeting my one contact, Yuri Kuntsevich, somewhere near the airport exit. I'm not proud to admit that my image of the Dyatlov Foundation president up to this point had been fairly cartoonish. I half expected to meet a bearded, unsmiling tank of a man who smelled faintly of vodka and cruciferous soup.

We exited the international terminal and were funneled into a crush of anxious drivers bearing signs of identification. I began to look for my own name, hunting for Roman lettering amid the Cyrillic, when two words in wobbly black marker caught our attention. The sign was unmistakable and, despite its dark meaning, I smiled when I read it: "Dyatlov Incident." On seeing Kuntsevich in the flesh, my image of the Russian hulk vaporized and was replaced by that of a kindly father figure. Kuntsevich was far into middle age—mid-sixties—but his remarkably square, doll-like face still clung to youth. On our approach, he smiled broadly and let the sign drop to his side. The three of us exchanged handshakes and brief hugs, but aside from some broken English on his part and a few shards of phrase-book Russian on ours, we said little.

Having been shunted from plane to plane for the previous twenty-six hours, I was desperate to step outside. It was still fall, and there was no snow on the ground yet, but the second we stepped into the early morning air, I craved heat. We followed our host to a Renault. But either the heater wasn't working in the car or the driver preferred not to use it. From the backseat, Jason and I listened to Kuntsevich speak insistent Russian into a cell phone that hung about his neck.

We traveled north to the city. Aside from the faint outline of smokestacks against the sky and the lights of the metropolis flickering in the distance, I could make out little else. For me, the city's significance revolved entirely around the Dyatlov hikers and the university, but for most first-time visitors, the place held the psychic residue of a very different tragedy. In 1918, after the three-centuries-old Romanov dynasty had fallen to control of the Bolsheviks the previous year, Czar Nicholas and his family were imprisoned in Yekaterinburg's Ipatiev House at the center of the city. In mid-July, as the country's civil war continued to roil and the anti-Communist White Army threatened to take back the city, the order was given to execute the entire royal family. In the early morning hours of July 17, the czar and czarina, along with their five children and various attendants, were brought to the building's basement where they were lined up—ostensibly for a family photograph—and executed at point-blank range. The scene was a protracted bloodbath. Those who did not die immediately by bullet were stabbed with bayonets. It would take yet another revolution, some seven decades later, before the Romanovs' remains would be recovered from a swamp outside the city. As I looked out at the lights of Yekaterinburg and to the imagined swampland beyond, I thought of how the family's bones had lain somewhere out there for decades, forgotten under a blanket of peat. Yet even after their bodies had been given a proper burial, the myths surrounding their deaths persisted—the most famous of which was that young Anastasia had escaped assassination to assume a new identity overseas. Russian conspiracy fabulists, it seems, never let facts get in the way of a good story.

When the buildings began to shift from grand neoclassical to boxy and austere, we were nearing Kuntsevich's working-class neighborhood. Everything was orderly, though there were hints of neglect and flourishes of graffiti. Once we entered Kuntsevich's complex, the smell of natural gas hit us like a wave. Intermittent fluorescents offered the only light, leaving slices of the hallway in shadow.

The two-bedroom apartment Kuntsevich shared with his wife was cozy—the modest space of a couple making do—and they were generous to accommodate us during our stay. We put on rubber slippers at the door and, as the sun rose, Kuntsevich's petite wife, Olga, set to work fixing an early breakfast. I watched her with an immediate fondness. Beneath her halo of dark hair, she had kind brown eyes and a sweet smile that reminded me of my late grandmother. The likeness made me feel close to this woman with whom I could barely communicate.

Olga led us to the kitchen where, on a table the size of a car tire, she served us piles of dark meat and root vegetables. Afterward, our host walked us down the street to the Military History Museum, where we took a brief tour of emasculated tanks, cannons and other artillery. We then got in the car and drove to the Mikhaylovskoye Cemetery at the center of town, where all but one of the hikers were buried. Kuntsevich, Jason and I crunched through dead leaves and undergrowth to the edge of the yard where eight marble headstones sat in a row along the border fence. Artificial lilies had been placed at each grave some time ago, and were now half-buried in leaves or weeds. Except for the names and years of birth, the stones were identical, and they all bore the same end: 1959. The

Krivonishchenko family had chosen to bury Georgy in a separate cemetery a few miles to the west, but Georgy was represented on a commemorative column nearby, on which nine black-and-white portraits had been preserved in marble. After a shared moment of silence, I took a few pictures and we made our way back over the neglected grounds to the car.

By midmorning, we were back in the car driving hours outside of town to the dense forest abutting the Ural Mountains. At this point, Jason and I had been awake for more than thirty hours and we couldn't figure out why, having just arrived in this country for the first time, Kuntsevich was taking us on what appeared to be an impromptu camping trip. Though we were on the verge of sleep-deprived delirium, Jason and I went along with the rest of the day's activities. We cut wood with a crosscut saw I thought only lumberjacks used. Over a campfire, we cooked a small bony fish that Kuntsevich had brought, and drank a batch of spiked fruit juice. I wondered if we would be pitching a tent next, but as night fell, Kuntsevich drove us back to the city. Perhaps this spontaneous excursion had been a kind of Russian endurance test, and our host had been assessing our stamina as outdoorsmen, and possibly as friends.

ON THE MORNING OF OUR SECOND DAY IN YEKATERINBURG, Kuntsevich summoned Jason and me into the downstairs apartment that he and his wife also owned. As we entered, he sat down at a small desk in the main room, surrounded by a giant heap of artifacts and documents on the Dyatlov case. Kuntsevich was wearing the same outfit as the previous day: a pinstriped jacket, mismatched pants, black socks and Russian sandals resembling Crocs. His cell phone, as ever, hung from his neck. After strapping a pair of jeweler's glasses to his head, he began to tinker with a small steel-framed device that sat on the desk.

Our host seemed to be in no hurry to fill us in on what he was doing—or perhaps he was being willfully obscure—so Jason and I took a seat on the couch and watched him. Finally, Kuntsevich aimed the desktop lamp in such a way that allowed us to get a somewhat better look at the device. It was an olive-green metal box embossed with an alligator pattern, and when I craned my neck I could see a metal device inside that resembled the head of a faucet. There was also some metal twine, and what appeared to be a large baize coaster. With surgical precision, using miniature tools, Kuntsevich toiled away for what must have been forty-five minutes, double-checking each part as if he were conducting a quality check on an assembly line. We were lacking a translator that day, so Jason and I had no choice but to sit there, watching our host work in the lengthening silence. We stole glances at each other, registering our growing discomfort and both wondering at what point we could just stand up and leave.

Then Kuntsevich began to hum, softly at first, then louder, as if he too were aware of the unbearable silence and was attempting to fill it. I didn't recognize the tune, though the melody sounded folksy. He then snuck a peak at us, a mischievous look telling us that he was enjoying every minute of his suspenseful stunt. He pulled open a drawer and produced what looked like a vinyl record. He placed the disc on the device, wound a crank on the side, and suddenly the music Kuntsevich had been humming was replaced by the real thing, issuing from the machine. The device was a phonograph.

Later, after our translator had arrived, Kuntsevich told us that this was the music that Igor and his friends had listened to and played for one another. "They were composing poems and stories and songs, and they would perform them for one another each night." When the song ended, Kuntsevich let the record skip and hiss for a full minute. He then replaced the record and set the needle on a new song. The wind-up nature of the player seemed to lend the mandolin, piano and folk guitar an additional layer of sadness and longing. It was a layer that I imagined only the three of us, sitting there fifty years after the hikers had listened to similar music, could detect.

OVER THE NEXT TWO DAYS, KUNTSEVICH ARRANGED FOR me to talk with various writers, armchair experts and other characters connected to the Dyatlov case, such as search volunteers and friends of the hikers. Though there was a translator present at each of these interviews, and I had arrived with lists of questions, I often left these meetings more confused than I'd gone in. I was learning that everyone had his or her own ideas as to what happened to the hikers, and none seemed to match the others. I was told tales of runaway murderous prison guards, top-secret military tests gone awry and a tale about mythic arctic dwarves. One man even alleged that the survivor Yuri Yudin had something to do with his friends' deaths—after all, wasn't it convenient that Yudin had gotten sick in the middle of the trip and had been forced to turn back? Might he have been complicit in a larger plot? Arctic dwarves aside, nearly all of these theories involved a deep distrust of the Soviet government and a belief that the euphemistic conclusion that the hikers had died of an "unknown compelling force" had been used to paper over a darker truth. Though I wasn't yet ruling anything out, by the end of these meetings, I knew that I needed to get to people who could give me facts, not more stories out of the *Fortean Times*.

DURING OUR DOWNTIME FROM INTERVIEWS ONE DAY, Kuntsevich, Jason and I explored the city in which the hikers had lived. I learned that Yekaterinburg—Sverdlovsk, to the Soviets—had been founded in 1723 as part of Peter the Great's effort to tap the riches of the Ural region. After the construction of the Trans-Siberian Railway in the late nineteenth century, the city had become a regional hub for mining, metallurgy and machine production. During the next century, the surrounding area became home to some of the largest and most brutal labor camps. Later known as *Gulags*—an acronym taken from the Russian name for the Chief Administration of Corrective Labor Camps—these camps were expanded by Stalin in the 1930s to house political prisoners, dissenters and other enemies of the State.

After making the historical rounds of the city by car, Kuntsevich pointed out the Ural State Technical University—or, as it was called until 1992, the Ural Polytechnic Institute. Westerners might know the university as the alma mater of former Russian president Boris Yeltsin; Igor Dyatlov and most of his friends would have been arriving just as Yeltsin was leaving in 1955. The proud columns and sculptured pediment of the campus's main building were already familiar to me from pictures I'd seen, and I was keen to explore the campus beyond the quad. After some purposeful wandering, we found the hikers' dormitory, which was closed to outsiders, but because Kuntsevich occasionally taught classes at the university, he was able to persuade a guard to let us into the building. We strolled the hallways, paying particular attention to the top-floor corridor, down which Igor and his friends had walked on the evening of their departure. I stuck my head into one of the open rooms. Quarters that might have been generously referred to as utilitarian in 1959, had slid into further neglect. I snapped a few photographs of peeling green paint and chipped stone tiles and we left.

As much as I was enjoying our city tour, by the end of the day, I was getting slightly anxious. When I asked Kuntsevich about contacting Yuri Yudin, he only shook his head or said, "I don't know." "You don't know where he is?" I pressed him. "I don't know," he would say again, and that would be that.

But on the morning of our fourth day, our host roused us from our foldout beds with news. In his now familiar patchwork of English, Russian and hand gestures, he explained that he had scheduled a meeting with Tatiana Dyatlov Dyatlova, Igor's little sister. I was thrilled. At last my quest was starting to seem real.

That afternoon, we took a train 30 miles west of the city to Pervouralsk, where Igor and his siblings had grown up and where Tatiana still lived. As we drew closer to her neighborhood, telephone wires multiplied over our heads, and red and white smokestacks coughed up a spectrum of grays and browns on the horizon. The sun had disappeared, but whether behind smoke or clouds, I couldn't make out. Whereas the graffiti had only flirted with Kuntsevich's neighborhood, it positively bloomed here, standing out as the main source of color amid cement and stone. Jason and I noted a passing rainbow of Cyrillic vandalism, speculating on what profanities it might contain.

Tatiana's building was a midcentury relic, with an exterior coat of paint that seemed to be in the middle of a decades-long process of detaching itself from the wall. We crunched through the moat of autumn leaves surrounding the complex and past a series of mangled mailboxes in order to reach the door. We passed more graffiti on our walk to a two-toned elevator. The right elevator door appeared to have been recently replaced, leaving the left door—painted an institutional green—stranded in the Soviet era. Across both doors was a splash of vandalism in the universal language of *Fuck You*.

After an unsteady ride to the third floor, we proceeded to an apartment at the end of the hall. We knocked and, after some rustling and barks, the door opened and I found myself face to face with the features that had become branded into my memory these past few months. She must have been in her early sixties, but Tatiana's resemblance to her brother was startling. Besides the shared eyes and sharp, Slavic cheekbones, there was the gap in her front teeth when she smiled. She promptly ushered us through the door, as if she were worried that someone in the hallway might be transcribing our conversation.

Her dog, a Jack Russell terrier, wouldn't stop barking, so Tatiana lifted the animal by its tail and pulled him into the next room. In contrast to what we'd seen of the building, her apartment was warm and pleasant. As we settled onto her pillowy couch, and I admired a painting above of a tranquil mountain lake, Tatiana hurried to set up tea. The table quickly disappeared under a spread of china, brass serving ware, cheese, fruit, pickles, jams, pastries and various sweets. I don't usually notice teapots, but the one she brought out was so striking that I wondered if it was a pre-Revolution antique. Kuntsevich casually plucked four sweets off a tray while we were waiting.

Our translator arrived, a shy girl in her early twenties. Tatiana began by expressing how happy she was that we had come, and how she considered us new friends. Yet I sensed a cautious diplomacy behind her warm welcome. I didn't want to overwhelm her, so I withheld my questions about her brother and instead made small talk about her country and our trip.

At last, between sips of heavily sugared tea, Tatiana broached the topic of her family and how their life had been before the tragedy. Besides Tatiana and Igor, there were two more siblings: their eldest brother, Slava, and, two years younger than Igor, their sister Rufina. But both had died years ago, leaving Tatiana the sole survivor.

All four Dyatlov children had been raised to be upstanding Communists, yet each had an independent spirit and inquiring mind, which they had parlayed into their respective fields of study. All four had attended UPI—Igor, Slava and Rufina for radio engineering, and Tatiana for chemical engineering. Tatiana told me that Igor had always been the most scientifically inclined of the siblings, as well as the most artistic. "He had an excellent knowledge of art,"

Igor Dyatlov using one of his handmade radios to communicate with another hiking group, 1957.

she said. "He was a great photographer. He used to love to play the guitar, as well—he'd write songs and poems, just for himself."

Through his love of photography, her brother had been able to combine his creative and technical appetites. He caught the photo bug early, and by the time he hit high school he was publishing his images in newspapers and magazines. He had also by this time turned his attention to technical invention. He built radio receivers, recording devices and even a makeshift telescope. "Igor made it possible for us to see the first Sputnik in 1957," Tatiana remembered. "We all went to the roof to witness this historic leap of scientific wonder."

Regarding her brother's enthusiasm for radios, she said, "One wall of Igor's room was completely covered with radio panels of active handmade radio receivers. He maintained shortwave communications with many radio fans, and, at the time, you couldn't buy a shortwave radio receiver—you had to build one."

As she told me this, I thought of how Igor's talent with radios had left followers of the Dyatlov case puzzled. Many couldn't understand why he had neglected to take a radio with him into the mountains, one he might have used to communicate with rescuers. But shortwave radios of the time were typically over a hundred pounds, and bringing one on a trip wasn't simply a matter of slipping it into a backpack. In his book *Everything Was Forever, Until It Was No More*, Soviet scholar Alexei Yurchak explains that Soviet policy toward shortwave radios at the time was "ambiguous," which may explain why young people like Igor were willing to take the risk. The radios may have been officially illegal, but their use wasn't entirely frowned upon. "Listening to foreign broadcasts was acceptable and even encouraged," Yurchak writes, "as long as these qualified as good cultural information and not bourgeois or anti-Soviet propaganda."

Tatiana told me that her brother had been an upstanding Communist and student. When he graduated from high school, he was honored with a silver medal that allowed him to enroll at any university in the country without taking an entrance exam. Part of being a star student, she explained, was adhering to communism like everyone else and believing that education and Party allegiance could elevate the entire country. "One has to remember, a new period of excitement was upon us. Young people wanted to get a higher education, to work in industry; they wanted to find themselves as well as something meaningful to do. The world was opening up around us in 1958, 1959. This was the first time—especially after such a brutal World War and subsequent sanctions and rationing—when people could buy a television or transistor radio."

But Igor's greatest passion was not school or even radios—it was the outdoors. He had developed a deep love of hiking over the years, having followed the example of his brother, Slava. "Slava was two years ahead of Igor, and his mentor," said Tatiana. "But Igor was a real leader and a true sportsman in his own right."

When I asked Tatiana what her last memory of Igor was, she said abruptly, "He didn't die from the snow." She then described seeing the open caskets at the funerals, and how darkly colored and aged their skin had been. "It's impossible. When people are just freezing and cold, the color of their face is not so dark." Of her brother's body, she said, "Igor was twenty-three years old and his hair looked like an old man's. It was white." Her family would not have believed it was Igor if not for one distinguishing mark on the corpse, one that brother and sister shared. "We knew it was Igor from the gap in his teeth . . . only the gap."

She stopped short of speculating what the aged appearance of her brother's body meant. "It's too difficult to find the truth. There are too many conflicting stories; so no one, in my opinion, will ever know."

I asked again what her final memory of her brother was. She told me how they had worked in tandem to develop a photograph he had taken of a mountain, one in the vein of Ansel Adams. "His photos were amazing," she said softly. She paused again before telling me that their mother had tried to talk Igor out of going on the trip. "My mother said to him, 'You must not go, you have exams and you need to graduate.' Igor replied, 'Mom, this is my last trip.' . . . For forty years, our mother lived with the fact that her son had died, and that the circumstances of his death were still unsolved, that we might never know the truth."

When Tatiana began to take things into the kitchen, I sensed our time was up. I would later notice a pattern with my interviews. Everything was friendly until it was suddenly over. Before we said good-bye, Tatiana left me with a final thought: "My mother's intuition was right. In 1994, before she died, all she remembered was that it was her fault."

On the train ride back to Kuntsevich's place, I couldn't get Dyatlov's mother out of my head. I wondered how many fretful mothers throughout history had been ignored by their obstinate children, only to see their nightmares realized. As if the loss weren't enough, these mothers were sentenced to a life of regret and of hearing the same refrain repeating uselessly in their heads: *I told you so*. With the birth of my own child imminent, the pain of Igor's mother tugged at my heart.

Igor Dyatlov was beginning to take real shape in my mind as a twentieth-century Renaissance man and adventurer. However, I knew that in order to create a fuller picture of the man and his final days, I would have to go beyond speaking with his sister—who, after all, had been only twelve years old at the time. I would have to talk to Yuri Yudin, the last person to see Igor and his friends alive. I found it difficult to believe that the president of the Dyatlov Foundation hadn't the slightest idea where the man was. But if Kuntsevich knew Yudin's whereabouts, he certainly wasn't telling me.

★

5

ON THE MORNING AFTER THEIR DEPARTURE, THREE HOURS before the lazy winter sun had risen, the Dyatlov group disembarked in Serov, an iron and steel manufacturing town 200 miles due north of Sverdlovsk. Blinov and his party joined them on the platform. It wasn't yet eight o'clock, and after ten and a half hours of gaiety and irregular sleep on the train, both hiking groups were weary. The next train, which was to take them to Ivdel, wasn't due to depart until evening, leaving the group of friends no choice but to spend the day in this unfamiliar mining town. Perhaps they could visit a local museum or—befitting their academic studies—a metallurgy plant.

Their first instinct was to get some sleep inside the station while it was still dark. They quickly discovered, however, that the doors were locked. The workers inside, speaking brusquely through the station windows, refused to allow any travelers in from the cold.

In classic fashion, Georgy lightened the mood by taking out his mandolin and breaking into song right there on the platform— a conspicuous disruption given the early hour and inhospitable surroundings. In comic imitation of a busker, he set out his felt cap for tips, his beanpole frame and protruding ears adding to the comedy of the moment. But his spontaneous merrymaking didn't last long because a nearby policeman heard the noise and strode over. Yudin recorded the incident in the group diary:

> *A policeman pricked up his ears; the town was all calm, no crime,*
> *no disturbances as if it's communism—and then Yu. Krivo started*
> *to sing, he was caught and taken away in no time.*

Without ceremony, Georgy was marched to the police station around the corner. His friends followed and watched as he was scolded by the sergeant.

> *A sergeant reminded Comrade Krivonishchenko that Article II.3*
> *of Internal Order at railway stations prohibits disturbing other*
> *passengers. It's the first station where songs are illegal, and the*
> *first one where we didn't sing.*

After a stern warning, Georgy was let go, at which point the friends retreated in the opposite direction from the police station, chewing over the details of Georgy's near arrest as they went. They planned to meet Blinov's team at the station that evening, which gave them the day to explore the town. Not far down a snow-paved road lined with log-cabin-style houses, the travelers encountered an elementary school, bearing the uninspired name of School #41. Desperate to find a place to catch up on their sleep, they knocked on the front door. A cleaning lady answered and, after hearing their predicament, allowed the group inside. They were soon greeted by a sympathetic schoolmaster, who agreed to let the hikers rest there if, in return, they would speak to his class later that day about their trip. The sleepy friends readily agreed to this new plan.

A typical Soviet school day was broken into two periods: a morning session devoted to proper lessons, followed by a less structured afternoon session, during which pupils could pursue their own activities or gather for guest speakers. Schoolchildren could

Local villagers in Serov,
January 24, 1959.

Alexander "Sasha" Zolotaryov in Serov. Photo taken by the
Dyatlov hikers, January 24, 1959.

typically expect war veterans, factory workers, museum docents or writers as afternoon guests. But a group of mountaineers who could regale them with their adventures? This was a rare thing.

With Igor and his friends well rested, they piled into a classroom of roughly thirty-five young faces, ranging in age from seven to nine. The little ones were eager to learn, and when the hikers revealed the contents of their backpacks, the children were held in captive fascination. There were ice crackers, maps, Zorki cameras and flashlights—known as "Chinese torches"—passed around the room. The guests even treated the class to a tent-pitching demonstration, and by the end, the children were begging to be taken along on future expeditions. With the educational portion of the visit concluded, the classroom erupted in song. The tattooed Sasha stepped forward with several new songs, including a Russified version of "Mary Had a Little Lamb" by Samuil Marshak. The song gave Sasha and the schoolchildren the opportunity to act out the verse.

Our Mary had a little lamb,
As loyal as a dog,
It always walked with her, yes ma'am,
Through thunder, storm, and fog.

When it was very, very young
She took it to the steppe,
But now, although it grew its horns,
It still walks in her step.

Say, Mary walks out of the gate,
The lamb walks after her.
She hops along the street, and what?
The lamb hops after her.

She reaches a corner, makes a right,
The lamb walks after her.
She shoots ahead with all her might,
It dashes after her.

While Sasha was certainly the star of the sing-along, the children fell hardest for Zina, and became emotional at the idea of her leaving them. They asked her to be the leader of the "Pioneers" — a youth group similar to the Scouts in the United States — not understanding that Zina couldn't stay. As evening drew near, the hikers wrapped up their visit with one last song, but the happy conclusion didn't prevent the children from becoming tearful when the hikers moved to leave. With their teacher's permission, the entire class poured out of the school and followed the ten adventurers down the road all the way to the train station. The kids pleaded with Zina again, begging her to stay and promising to be well behaved if she would only agree to remain behind and lead their children's group.

The hikers said their final good-byes to the children and boarded the 6:30 PM train bound for Ivdel. As they took their seats — and Lyuda prepared to disappear beneath hers — the travelers assumed their adventures in Serov had come to an end. But there was one final incident awaiting them in the train car, a peculiar one given that none of the hikers drank alcohol. Yudin recorded the incident in the group diary:

In the carriage, some young drunkard demanded we give him a half-liter bottle, claiming we'd stolen it from his pocket. That's the second time today the story ended with interference of a policeman.

After the disruption resolved itself, the hikers were left most vividly with the impression of the classroom they had visited that day — and the love the schoolchildren had so readily given them.

Weeks later, once School #41 had gotten word that the Dyatlov group was missing, the children all wrote letters to UPI, expressing their concern and asking the frank questions that children ask. *What happened to their new friends? Where was Zina?* But their mail went unanswered, even after the group's fate was known. Yuri Yudin received one such letter from a child they had met that day, but he didn't have the heart to write back. What could he say?

★

6

ON FEBRUARY 20, THE SAME DAY A SEARCH HELICOPTER
is dispatched from Sverdlovsk, the Ivdel prosecutor's office orders
a criminal investigation into the case of the missing hikers. There
is nothing yet criminal to investigate, but the purview of the
office goes beyond the strictly criminal. The regional prosecutor,
Nikolay Klinov, assigns prosecutor Vasily Tempalov to head up
the investigation, most likely because Tempalov's Ivdel office is
closest to where the hikers were last seen. Tempalov holds the title
of junior counselor of justice—the equivalent rank of major in the
army—and though at thirty-eight years he is relatively young, he
has considerable experience prosecuting cases in the region. He
has zero experience, however, with young hikers gone missing,
and until the searchers turn up some evidence of the hikers, there
is little Tempalov can do from his office.

The Sports Committee of Sverdlovsk, meanwhile, is trying to
determine the hikers' route so that they can relay the information
to the search teams. Because Igor Dyatlov's intended course was
not found in the hiking commission's files, the committee will have
to track down someone acquainted with the group's journey. Not
realizing that one of the hikers, Yuri Yudin, has since returned to
town, the committee turns to the only man they believe can help:
Yevgeny Maslennikov, chief mechanical engineer at the local Verkh-
Isetsky Metal Mill. Not only is he a distinguished UPI alumnus,

he is also one of the best backcountry skiers in the city and serves as a hiking consultant to clubs throughout the larger region of Sverdlovsk. In fact, he personally signed off on Igor Dyatlov's proposed course into the northern Urals.

When Maslennikov receives a call from Valery Ufimtsev of the Municipal Sports Committee, he is surprised to learn that Igor and his friends have not yet returned. "I told him what I knew about their route," Maslennikov later told investigators. "I said that the route was hard, but the group was strong; they couldn't lose their way, and therefore the situation is critical."

After relaying the group's intended destination of Otorten Mountain, Maslennikov suggests to Ufimtsev that one of the hikers may have a leg injury that has slowed the entire group. Or, he speculates, they all caught the flu and are recovering in a nook somewhere. Before Maslennikov hangs up, he agrees to join the growing search efforts as an adviser. Three days later, he would himself fly to Ivdel to join the air and ground searches.

Gordo and Blinov, meanwhile, have been unsuccessful in their attempts to pick up the hikers' trail leading from Bahtiyarova village. By the estimates of Mansi villagers, the hikers had arrived approximately sixteen days earlier, putting their visit around February 4.

On February 23, the day after Gordo and Blinov visit the village, several Mansi tribesmen join the search effort. Their help is essential, as the Mansi know these mountains intimately. The group is headed by Stepan Kurikov, who, despite his Russian name, is a respected elder of his people. It is not unusual for the partially assimilated Mansi to take Russian names.

By now the search teams have arranged for radiograms to be sent back to Ivdel and Sverdlovsk. The radio is heavy and requires skilled operators, but this wireless form of communication is the only way to send messages rapidly between the mountains and the city hundreds of miles away. The first radiogram reads:

```
MANSI AGREE TO JOIN SEARCH
DAILY PAYMENT FOR 4 MEN 500 RUBLES
MANSI FOUND TRACKS 90 KM FROM SUYEVATPAUL TOWARD
  URAL RIDGE
GIVE PERMISSION FOR SEARCH

                                        /BARANOV/
```

Upon Maslennikov's arrival in Ivdel on February 24, there is a noticeable escalation in the search efforts. The same day, the Ivdel municipality agrees to a search of all possible routes the Dyatlov group may have taken. In addition to continued aerial sweeps, there are new boots hitting the ground, among them UPI students, family members, local officials and volunteers from the surrounding work camps. Over the next few days, nearly thirty searchers fan out over the snowy topography, targeting the Vishera River in the Perm region, Otorten Mountain itself, the Auspiya River valley, and the surrounding areas of Oyko-Chakur and Sampal-Chahl.

A search by helicopter over the Auspiya River is quick to pick up ski tracks along the bank. Groups on the ground, meanwhile, follow up on the discovery of Mansi hunters that ski tracks and evidence of camping were spotted 55 miles from the Mansi village of Suyevatpaul. In response to the latter, a group headed by the Mansi team's Stepan Kurikov, accompanied by a radio operator, sets out in the direction of the ski path. In anticipation of finding the hikers at the end of these tracks, they equip themselves with a first aid kit and food.

By the next day, however, there is still no immediate sign of the hikers. One of the groups, headed by UPI student Boris Slobtsov, is searching the Lozva River valley when a message drops to them from overhead. Aerial note-dropping is a common form of communication, particularly in remote areas where radio transmission is difficult or impossible. The communication can work both ways.

Helicopter search for the hikers, February 1959.

Members of the search team gather to strategize. (From left to right: Mikhail Sharavin, Vladimir Strelnikov, Boris Slobtsov and Valery Khalezov.) Photo taken by Vadim Brusnitsyn, February 1959.

For the searchers to relay to airplane or helicopter pilots that everything is fine, two people lie parallel in the snow. To indicate the direction they are headed, four people form the shape of an arrow. If a message needs to be communicated to searchers on the ground, a note is attached to a brightly colored object, often red, which flaps visibly on its descent.

The note dropped to Boris Slobtsov on February 25 instructs the party to alter its route and begin searching along a smaller adjacent river, the Auspiya, where ski tracks were recently spotted. Slobtsov and his team of nine promptly change course and that same day pick up not only on the Dyatlov ski trail, but also evidence of one of their campsites along the river.

Boris Slobtsov is not a trained searcher, nor is anyone else in his group. He is twenty-two years old, in his third year of studies at UPI and is a member of the hiking club. He not only admires Igor Dyatlov as a fellow hiker, but also considers him a friend. If something like this could happen to someone as capable as Dyatlov, it could happen to any one of them. It was a fellow hiker's duty to help in any way that he could.

Slobtsov's group sets up camp that night in the protection of the neighboring forest, planning to reconnect with the ski tracks the next day. The next morning, however, as they resume their course along the river, Slobtsov and his crew are unable to pick up the trail. The wind that day is strong, and it is easy to imagine that the tracks have simply blown away. The wind is so fierce in this region, Slobtsov notes, that the straps on his ski poles often lie parallel to the ground. With no trail to follow, the searchers have no choice but to continue along the river.

One of the searchers in his group, a volunteer named Ivan, complains of feeling ill and informs Slobtsov that he will be turning back to Ivdel. Though the group believes he isn't sick at all, only scared, they agree to go on without him. Before Ivan leaves, he suggests that the group continue in the direction of Otorten

Otorten Mountain, the destination of the Dyatlov hikers.
Photograph taken by the rescue team, February 1959.

Mountain until they encounter a streambed at the bottom of a slope. Because of the westerly wind in this area, he says, the snow has accumulated along the slope, creating potential avalanche conditions. The possibility that Dyatlov and his friends have gotten buried in snow is not one Slobtsov wants to believe, but after the group says good-bye to Ivan, they take his advice and head in the direction of the mountain. To increase their chances of success, Slobtsov suggests the team break into pairs, with Slobtsov taking classmate and hiking-club member Mikhail Sharavin. From the Auspiya River, Slobtsov and Sharavin head up the slope, hoping to get a better view from the hill overlooking the riverbed. By now, the weather is worsening and their time is limited.

At some point in the afternoon, before they are able to reach the crest of the hill, Sharavin sees something that makes his pulse quicken. "About seventy meters to our left," Sharavin remembered later, "I noticed a black spot that was actually part of a tent."

Sharavin alerts Slobtsov, and the young men hurry toward the spot as quickly as the wind and deep snow will allow them. The tent's poles are still vertical, with the south-facing entrance still standing. But recent snowfall has covered much of the tarpaulin, causing part of it to collapse—though it is not immediately clear whether this is the result of a storm, or of wind redistributing the surrounding snow. The men call out but receive no answer. There is an ice ax near the front of the tent, sticking out of the snow. There is also a partially buried Chinese torch, left in the on position. Sharavin retrieves the ax. He swings it behind him and brings it forward to rip open the tent.

★

7

2012

MY TRIP TO RUSSIA HAD NOT PROVIDED THE RESOLUTION I had hoped. At least I had earned Yuri Kuntsevich's trust, despite the language barrier. He had led me to Tatiana and, after that, had set up a meeting with Lyuda's brother, Igor—a man of few words, as it turned out. I later found out that Igor passed away not long after I interviewed him. The circle of people who had known the hikers was becoming smaller all the time.

Before I left Russia, Kuntsevich had transferred the entire Dyatlov case file to my laptop—452 digital pages, entirely in Russian. The case records had been available for viewing only since the late 1980s, when Gorbachev's glasnost called for increased transparency of government activities. It wasn't until the late '90s that partial copies of the case—having been illegally smuggled out of the Sverdlovsk Regional State Archives—revived interest in the Dyatlov tragedy. But this incomplete copy of the case file was largely used by writers to sensationalize the tragedy, much to the exasperation of the Yekaterinburg prosecutor's office. Additional clandestine photocopies continued to circulate into the new millennium, but it wasn't until 2009 that stealthy copiers, most likely students, pieced together a comprehensive reproduction of the case and distributed it among a select number of enthusiasts.

Besides the case file, Kuntsevich had also given me nearly five hundred photographs and negatives courtesy of Lev Ivanov's daughter, Alexandra. She had been just a toddler when her father was appointed lead investigator to the case, and in 2009 she donated her father's long-forgotten photo archive to the Dyatlov Foundation. While still in Russia, Jason and I had rushed to get the negatives printed. Once we had the prints in hand, we were faced with images more upsetting than I had been prepared for—the most disturbing of which were photographs from the Ivdel morgue of the hikers' still-frozen bodies awaiting autopsy.

Why should anyone in Russia trust me? Why, as Kuntsevich had asked me, did I care so much about nine hikers who had died in a foreign country five decades ago? I couldn't answer these questions to anyone's satisfaction, least of all my own.

For over a year, I pored over the translated case files and the hikers' journals, and many hours of my own transcribed interviews, as well as sought any other information on the case that I could find. When I felt I had exhausted these sources, I booked another flight to Russia. If I couldn't find Yuri Yudin, I could at the very least put myself in the place of Igor Dyatlov and his friends. I would embark on the hikers' expedition, starting out from the Yekaterinburg train station and concluding on the remote slope in the northern Ural Mountains where they had died.

I communicated my plans to Kuntsevich via e-mail. He didn't seem particularly surprised by my proposal, but then his e-mails were always matter-of-fact. He agreed not only to host a second visit, but also to accompany me on my trek and to arrange for guides to take us deep into the mountains. When I asked him yet again how I might track down Yuri Yudin, his response gave me slim hope: *I will try.* When I asked him what gear I should bring, he wasn't any more specific than: *Bring warm clothes.* When I inquired where we would be staying on our hike, he wrote: *In a snow igloo.* Was he serious? Was I? His succinct responses and my inability to interpret them were starting to drive me slightly crazy. But what else could I do but trust him? I began my trip preparations.

When one lives in the Mediterranean climate of the Los Angeles basin, preparing for an excursion of subarctic temperatures takes some imagination. Whenever I was torn between two items— *Gore-Tex or Polartec?*—I had to remind myself that Igor Dyatlov and his friends hadn't been afforded the luxury of such conundrums. Their idea of "windproofing" had been to add another sweater under their jackets. And if they needed weather-resistant footwear, the only option was to sew their own boot covers. Even so, I spent an obscene amount of time and money on purchasing warm items for the trip: a wool hat with earflaps; two pairs of Gore-Tex gloves; woolen socks; Gore-Tex oversocks; long underwear; a fleece-lined, seal-colored Patagonia midlayer jacket; a military-issued outer jacket; and, my proudest purchase, my "Arctic Pro" model boots, insulated with thermal foam and encased in rubber. I was so pleased with my new boots that when they arrived, I brought them to a send-off lunch with some friends, informing them how warm my feet would be in temperatures as low as −60 degrees Fahrenheit. I even urged my friends to take turns trying them on in the restaurant.

Before I left, I received a final e-mail from Kuntsevich containing a few details on my brief layover in Moscow. The e-mail would have been unsurprising had it not been for a sentence thrown in at the bottom: *Yuri Yudin sends his greetings.* I had temporarily given up on the hunt to track down the Dyatlov group's only survivor, and I wasn't sure how to respond to this cryptic bit of information. Had Kuntsevich really tracked down Yudin, or was Yudin simply sending a message from his place of hiding? Rather than try to resolve this over e-mail, I decided to save my questions for when I saw Kuntsevich in person.

Soon I was on another fifteen-hour flight headed east. I was alone this time, but there was something else that was different about this trip: At thirty-nine years old, I was now a father. My girlfriend, Julia, had given birth a year earlier—on February 1—to our beautiful son, Dashiel. For the rest of my life there would be this invisible string tying me to my family, tugging at the first sign of danger, warning me not to leave my son minus a parent. All that protective gear in my suitcase was not so much to protect myself, as it was to protect someone far more vulnerable. Julia's unswerving support, and her insistence that I make this second trip, had certainly helped settle my nerves, but an investigation into the Dyatlov case wasn't the sort of endeavor that allayed one's fears of unforeseen disaster.

Kuntsevich would again be waiting for me at the Yekaterinburg airport, but he was sending someone to meet me during my Moscow layover—a man named Vladimir Borzenkov. As was typical of our exchanges, Kuntsevich had told me little about Borzenkov, other than that the man would be acting as "my attorney." I wasn't sure what that meant, or why I would need an attorney. Before I left, Kuntsevich had provided me with a snapshot of Borzenkov: a middle-aged man in a white hat.

Once we landed at Moscow's Sheremetyevo airport, I made my way through security, laptop in tow. I was now traveling with several hundred pages of case files on my laptop, and in my ever-increasing paranoia, I had created aliases for my Dyatlov-case folders. "Dyatlov" was now "Dash," my son's nickname. I had even created a decoy folder on my desktop labeled "Russia Trip 2012," complete with touristy excursions dug up on websites and my plans for visiting the famous Kungur Ice Caves, which I had no intention of seeing. Until I knew more about the case, I didn't think it wise to go trumpeting to the Russian authorities my real reason for being in their country. I can't be sure if my complex system of folder aliases was a stroke of genius or simply the result of having read too many John le Carré novels.

After some of the crowds around the baggage carousel had dispersed, I noticed a man, probably in his sixties, standing alone against one wall, gripping a briefcase in both hands. He had closely trimmed white hair and a mismatched suit—black pinstriped jacket paired with navy pants. He looked more like a writer or academic than an attorney.

I approached him hesitantly. "Excuse me, Vladimir Borzenkov?" He stepped forward. "Donnie?" We shook hands, and between my meager Russian and his halting English, we agreed to make our way to the nearest airport café. As we walked, I noticed a dark skeleton key bobbing from a cord around his neck. This detail might have puzzled me had I not already gathered from my last trip that (A) skeleton keys were still widely in use in Russia, and (B) Russians were fond of wearing keys and cell phones around their necks, where they were less likely to be lost or stolen.

We arrived at an empty café and sat down at a corner booth. Before I could drop my luggage and settle into my seat, Borzenkov had undone the lock on his high-security briefcase. Within seconds the table was covered in maps, hand-drawn diagrams, and what he told me were declassified government documents—all in Russian, of course. I adopted a pose of intense interest, poring over the pile even though I couldn't understand a word of what I was looking at. I took out my laptop, but the lack of Wi-Fi in the airport prevented me from resorting to Google Translate. Borzenkov opened his own laptop, a bulky antique, and pecked out a string of words into what looked to be crude translation software. After five minutes of this, we'd gotten nowhere.

To ease the awkward silences, I offered to buy him a warm drink or a candy bar, but he shook his head and continued to barrel through the mountains of data. Despite my inability to understand 90 percent of what he was saying, and the fact I hadn't slept in twenty-six hours, I had no doubt that he was giving me insights into the Dyatlov case. The man's dedication to the incident was clear, and I was deeply grateful for his time.

After two hours of frustrating back-and-forth, I stopped trying to understand him and simply watched his expressions. I again tried to offer him something to eat or drink from the café, but he refused. I then produced an energy bar from my backpack, which he accepted. He studied its gummy consistency like a scientist, opening the wrapper carefully and taking a hesitant bite before promptly placing it in his briefcase.

When it was time for me to catch my connecting flight to Yekaterinburg, we said our good-byes, and I thanked my "attorney" profusely in Russian. Though what I was thanking him for exactly, I wasn't sure. As I headed to my gate with a final wave, I was fairly certain that I would never see Vladimir Borzenkov again.

I ARRIVED AT THE YEKATERINBURG AIRPORT JUST AFTER 3:00 AM. Despite my crushing jet lag, I was delighted to see Yuri Kuntsevich's smiling face. It was over a year since we'd last seen each other. No sooner had we exchanged hugs than he took the phone dangling from his neck and began to talk into it. He appeared to be in the middle of some heavy negotiation, though what he could be negotiating at three in the morning, I could only guess. Was he comparing notes with Borzenkov? I soon found out he was just trying to find our driver.

Outside, there was snow on the ground and a pervasive sense of early-morning calm. As I stood with Kuntsevich waiting for our car, I drew in deep lungfuls of icy air. It felt right to be back. When the car dropped us at Kuntsevich's apartment, I was greeted by the familiar odor of fossil fuel. Inside the apartment, Olga was awake and preparing breakfast for us. Her face brightened when we entered, and after a warm hug, she was ready with an English greeting: "Good to see you again" and "You are like family." She had clearly been practicing.

I swapped my shoes for rubber slippers, and within five minutes of our arrival the three of us were seated around the compact kitchen table. The space was so cozy that Olga didn't have to get up from her chair to serve the food from the counter or stove. She simply swiveled and grabbed what she needed. Russian political radio filled the air as we ate chicken wrapped in foil, with potatoes, cabbage and sour cream.

As we neared the end of the meal, Olga surprised me with yet more of her English vocabulary. I was touched by her efforts, and was starting to feel ashamed that I hadn't learned more Russian. But I quickly forgot my guilt when I understood what she was trying to communicate in her earnest, overenunciated English. She and her husband, she said, had a guest staying downstairs in the spare apartment. He had arrived the previous day. The guest was Yuri Yudin.

★

8

2012

KUNTSEVICH AND I HEADED DOWN TO THE LOWER FLAT, where Yuri Yudin was staying. I'd spent time in the unit on my first visit, and had come to think of it, in its role as the Dyatlov Foundation offices, as "ground zero" for the case. Now, as Kuntsevich unlocked the door, I saw the main room's assemblage of evidence through the eyes of Yudin: the cracked bamboo ski poles, Zorki 35mm cameras, clothing, tent materials, drawers of case files, maps, as well as scores of photos from the 1959 rescue effort. I wondered how he felt about sleeping here, among the belongings of his fallen comrades.

Kuntsevich went to the corner and roused his guest from his bed on the couch. Yudin arose sleepily and held out his hand in greeting. He stood at about five-foot-seven and had a full head of spiky gray hair. There was something delicate about the way he moved, even for a man in his mid-seventies, reminding me of his various lifelong ailments. We shook hands before he shuffled into the kitchen to make tea.

I had worried that it might be difficult for him to talk about the tragedy, and indeed, when Yudin returned to the room, my fears were confirmed. Through our translator, he explicitly laid down the rules for our conversation. The focus of the story should not be about him, he said, and everything about the tragedy had already been told. He then turned his clear, slate-blue eyes toward me: "Do you not have mysteries in your own country that are unsolved?" Of course I did. What could I say? In lieu of an answer, I smiled and suggested we sit down at a table in the center of the room. He picked up my tape recorder and examined it with curiosity. Yudin then told me something that had not occurred to me. Today was February 27, fifty-three years ago to the day that the first bodies of the hikers had been discovered.

It was Yudin who started with the questions: Which picture do you want to paint? The one rooted in the Revolution, or that of the Iron Curtain? Puzzled, I told him that while the political backdrop of the time certainly interested me, I wasn't looking for a political angle on the story. But, because he appeared to be expecting me to choose, I stammered something about the Iron Curtain being of interest. This answer appeared to please him and he began.

Outdoor exploration had been a huge part of young Soviets' lives in the late '50s, Yudin said, and hikers like the Dyatlov group had used expeditions to escape the confines of big cities. "After Stalin died," he said, "things opened up more, and students could go almost anywhere within the country. But we still couldn't go abroad." To Yudin and his friends, the next best thing to international travel had been escaping into the wilderness, which held a romance all its own. Yet at the same time, domestic *tourists* were providing a useful service in helping to map out uncharted regions of the country, particularly Siberia and the Ural Mountains.

Fraternity, equality and respect were considered the reigning values among Russian hikers. "If someone was not friendly or did not work well within the group, they were not invited back," Yudin said. Furthermore, women were on equal footing with men. In his view, unlike the culture then prevalent in the United States—where women's careers hadn't advanced much beyond their prewar positions as telephone operators, schoolteachers and secretaries—there were fewer limitations on women of the Soviet Union at the time.

This equality was reflected in the Dyatlov group, where Zina and Lyuda were considered as capable as their male counterparts. "Within the team there was no gender. We were all equal in everything. We had a strict code of ethics and discipline. At that time, the most important goal was the spirit of being together as a team, and overcoming the distance."

Given Yudin's rheumatism and the accompanying arthritic symptoms that had plagued him since childhood, his decision to join the Dyatlov group may have seemed counterintuitive. But the challenges that came with hiking and mountaineering allowed him to better cope with his chronic condition, both mentally and physically. The very illness that had driven him to the sport, and had potentially put Yudin in harm's way, had also, in his words, become his "salvation."

To my surprise, talk of his illness led Yudin to open up about his poor childhood, which was spent in the town of Emelyashevka, a half-day's drive outside of Yekaterinburg. During the summers he had walked barefoot outside so that he could preserve his only pair of shoes for the winter months. In instances where he had to wear shoes at his destination, he would tie them to a stick and carry them over his shoulder as he walked. During the Second World War, food rations were the norm. "I tried sugar for the first time when I came to school," he told me. "I was seven and it was wartime, and nobody had anything. The government was giving us a loaf of bread and a teaspoon of sugar, which we'd spread out on the bread."

Yudin's much older brother served as an aviator during the war and survived. Their father also served, but was not so lucky. His death left Yudin's illiterate mother to care for him and his older sister. It was a difficult time, Yudin said, but conditions improved for his family when his brother returned from the war and was able to segue into a teaching career.

The post-Stalinist period came with new opportunities for Yudin's generation, including wider access to education. After the Dyatlov tragedy, Yudin went on to earn his degree in geology from UPI. After attending graduate school for economics, he moved north to Solikamsk, a mining city in the Perm district, where he settled into a career as an engineer in a magnesium plant. Yudin worked at the same Solikamsk plant his entire life before his retirement from factory life in the late '90s.

After the tragedy, Yudin's rheumatism abated enough for him to continue enjoying the outdoors. Yudin has retained his love of hiking and has continued to organize trips into the Urals. "It's a university tradition which carries on," he said proudly. "Hiking has always been my hobby. And of course what happened in 1959 was a horrible thing, but it's what I do."

Talk turned to the upcoming expedition, which was still over a week away. Kuntsevich interrupted our conversation to inform us that weather conditions in the northern Ural Mountains were going to be very unpredictable. Sudden blizzards and violent winds were a real threat, and a clear sky could lull one into a false sense of security. And once you're above the tree line, there's no place to seek cover. I nodded my understanding that I was aware of the dangers. But if his intention was to spook me, he had succeeded. I reluctantly wrapped up my talk with Yudin for the day, and we made a plan to resume the following morning.

That night after dinner, I slipped out of the apartment in search of a beer to soothe my growing agitation. I found a bar within ten minutes, tucked below street level in the subbasement of a concrete building. The three beers I ended up drinking there were a bad idea, and by the time I left the cigarette-choked bar and was walking home, a strange paranoia overtook me. Kuntsevich had found out earlier in the day that the car hired to pick me up at the airport a few days prior had been deliberately banged up after dropping me off. Kuntsevich theorized that the FSB, the modern equivalent of the KGB, had damaged the hired car as a warning for me to stop looking into the case. I had found Kuntsevich's Cold War–level of paranoia amusing, endearing even, but as I walked home that night, it seemed that everyone I passed on the street was looking at me a beat too long. What if Kuntsevich was right, and I wasn't welcome here? I hurried back to the apartment, touched to find that Olga had stayed up past her bedtime to make sure I returned safely.

★

9

JANUARY 25, 1959

WHEN THE TEN HIKERS ARRIVED IN IVDEL, IT WAS STILL dark, and a half-day's wait lay ahead of them for their next means of transportation. For those traveling from Sverdlovsk, a ski-hiking excursion into the Urals meant several days of assorted travel in order to get anywhere near the point where they would begin using their skis. And because the railway deviated east from Ivdel, the group would have to take a bus to continue north to Vizhay. There, at their last civilized outpost, they would have a chance to send out any final dispatches before slipping off the radar.

Once again, Yuri Blinov and his group were shadowing Igor and his friends. Blinov, who would later become a devoted member of the search team, wrote in his diary of this period, "Together we went through all the transitions between trains, buses and trucks in Serov, Ivdel and Vizhay. In other words, on our way we still communicated like members of the same hiking team." After spending the night at the Ivdel train station—a far more obliging terminal, as it turned out, than its counterpart in Serov—the hikers caught a tram to Ivdel proper. Situated at the junction of the Ivdel and Lozva rivers, the town existed first as a gold-mining settlement, and later as the location of the Ivdellag—a Soviet prison camp built in 1937.

Unknown to most Westerners until the 1963 English-language publication of Alexander Solzhenitsyn's *One Day in the Life of Ivan Denisovich*—and, later, *The Gulag Archipelago*—Stalin's ramped-up secret prison system had only been rumored to exist at this time. In fact, the Gulag system predated Hitler's concentration camps and would go on to function for many decades after the liberation of Buchenwald and Auschwitz. It wasn't until 1989 that Gorbachev finally began to reform the Soviet prison system.

But on their brief stay in the town, the young hikers would see none of the Soviet dissidents exiled to this region; they were focused entirely on readying themselves for their own temporary exile into the Russian wild. At the moment, this meant waiting at the Ivdel bus station. For the men, this would have been an ideal moment to break out the cigarettes and let their lungs fill with the heat of burning tobacco. But, as Zina liked to remind them, they had made a pact not to smoke, and no one had brought any cigarettes. So as they stood in the cold, the only smoke issuing from their mouths was their breath hitting the air.

At last, a small GAZ-651 rolled up. GAZ was a Soviet make of buses and trucks that had been mass-produced since the end of World War II. This particular bus most likely doubled as a transporter to shuttle local workers to and from the camps, but today it was a *tourist* bus. The GAZ had only twenty-five seats, and with the hikers alone numbering twenty, and a handful of locals needing seats of their own, the only solution was to pile baggage and people on top of one another.

If this had been the city, the driver might have felt compelled to turn away the backpackers, but camaraderie forms quickly in small towns, and everyone involved was determined to make it work. As the bus left Ivdel, the travelers were balanced comically on several layers of backpacks, skis and each other. "Top-layer passengers sat on chairbacks," the Dyatlov group's diary recounted, "with their legs on the shoulders of comrades." But their discomfort didn't stop Georgy from filling the air with the strumming of his mandolin, or his fellow passengers from singing along, as Ivdel receded through the windows.

The two-hour bus ride was an "express" of sorts, stopping only for bathroom breaks. In rural parts of the country—as is still in practice in Russia today—bathroom stops were at the whim of the bus driver, and when he pulled over, the doors were thrown open to the collective urinal of the roadside. Women filed along the left side of the bus, while the men went to the right.

At one of the more comfortable rest stops along the way, the bus to Vizhay parked near a shop, which allowed the passengers to stray farther from the bus and for longer than was usual. Because the vehicle was such a muddled heap of baggage and passengers, after it finally pulled away, it took the hikers some time to realize that someone was missing from their ranks: *Where's Kolevatov?*

It was certainly unlike the disciplined Kolevatov to have missed his ride. Was it possible that he had slipped away for an illicit smoke break? "He was always smoking an antique pipe during hikes," Yudin later remembered his friend, "fuming everyone with an aroma of real tobacco."

None of the hikers would have thought to keep tabs on Kolevatov because he tended to look out for himself. Yudin describes him as being a careful person, bordering at times on pedantic. But Kolevatov's reputation had soared among those at the university's hiking club the previous summer after his return from a hiking excursion into Siberia. The trip had taken Kolevatov's group along the Kazyr River and through a particularly challenging section of the Bazybay rapids. When their raft overturned, and nearly all of their belongings were lost, it was Kolevatov's foresight that saved the lives of his group: He was the only one to have properly secured his pack to the raft. Because he had the sole pack of flour and book of matches, he saved the group from starvation.

Whereas one of the other passengers might have been forced to stay behind to wait for the next day's bus, the intrepid Kolevatov wouldn't let his mistake ruin the trip. He did the only thing he could: He ran. The driver had a schedule to keep and couldn't alter his route or turn the bus around, but he agreed to wait. The hikers peered out the bus windows until they could see the figure of their friend sprinting toward them. Though Yudin doesn't recall why Kolevatov missed the bus, he remembers how frightened his friend looked at having been nearly abandoned. When he boarded the bus, "His eyes were bulging from his head."

Years later, Yudin couldn't help but wonder what would have happened if they had neglected to notice his absence until later. "Maybe he would have had to turn back, to wait the next day for the bus to Vizhay. The entire group would have been delayed by a day. It is difficult not to wonder: How would it have changed things?"

At two o'clock that afternoon, the bus arrived in Vizhay, a sizable woodcutting settlement complete with a school, hospital, shops and even a community center that screened movies. The town had been built on the backs of Gulag prisoners and free workmen of the area, both of whom would be sent out into the forests by day and return to their respective camps at night. Because the prison camps were kept strictly separate from the town, none of the hikers saw any prisoners during their stay in Vizhay, but, as detailed in Blinov's diary on the day of their arrival, they did see members of the free workers' camps: "On that day, a meeting of young Communist party members from all work camps was held and was coming to an end when we arrived. After the meeting, young Communists were transported to their camps."

Happily for Blinov's party, they happened to meet a group of these workers who were driving back to their encampment, Sector 105, for the night, the exact direction in which Blinov and his friends were headed. The Dyatlov group, for their part, wouldn't be able to hitch a ride to their next destination until the following morning. They would have to spend the night in Vizhay.

The two groups enjoyed their remaining time together by getting a late lunch at a local cafeteria, one frequented by the area's woodcutters. There, according to Kolevatov's journal, they

Zinaida "Zina" Kolmogorova at the group's Vizhay accommodations, January 26, 1959.

enjoyed a final meal "in a warm, friendly circle." The Vizhay cafeteria wasn't quite warm enough to inspire the shedding of outerwear, but it did provide the students a homey atmosphere and hot food. The travelers gathered at several tables near the windows, and between servings of bread and stew, they spread out maps, journals and last-minute projects on the plaid tablecloths. Zina, who was already anticipating foul weather ahead, got to work with a needle and thread making *bahily*, boot covers made out of a weather-resistant tarpaulin.

Later, the Dyatlov and Blinov groups assembled for a final photograph before parting ways. Then Blinov and his party climbed into the truck with the Sector 105 workers and waved farewell to their classmates, confident they would see them back at school the following month. But it was there, Yuri Blinov later wrote, that "we saw Dyatlov's group for the last time."

The Dyatlov hikers in Vizhay cafeteria: Alexander Kolevatov (far left under mirror), Yuri "Georgy" Krivonishchenko (right of mirror), Igor Dyatlov (back against wall) and Nikolay "Kolya" Thibault-Brignoles (back against window), January 26, 1959.

The Dyatlov hikers gather with their friends to say good-bye for the last time, January 26, 1959.

The Dyatlov hikers' tent one day after it was found. Vladislav
Karelin (left) and Yuri Koptelov (right). The search team's
activities in and around the tent, combined with recent
snowfall, have caused the canvas to collapse. February 27, 1959.

★

10

THERE ARE NO BODIES IN THE TENT. FOR BORIS SLOBTSOV and Mikhail Sharavin this means that there is a chance their schoolmates are still alive, perhaps holed up in a cave or shelter somewhere. The careful arrangement of items in the tent, including food ready for consumption, contributes to a sense of normalcy and give the pair further cause for optimism. If it were not for the partially collapsed tarpaulin, they might have supposed Igor and his friends were there only moments before.

The two men step outside of the tent to consider their next move. As they scan the surrounding landscape, snow begins to fall, and they realize it is probably too late to search the area. Before heading back to camp, they gather items that may prove useful to the search party: a jacket, a camera, the medicinal alcohol, a pair of skis, Igor's Chinese torch and the ice ax.

When the men reach camp, they find that the chief radio operator, Igor Nevolin, has since arrived with the rest of his group. Now that they can communicate via radio, Slobtsov has a radiogram sent off to investigators in Ivdel breaking the news of their discovery. The message reveals the location of the tent—on the eastern slope, at a height of 1,079 meters—and explains that further investigation has been suspended due to an approaching snowstorm. A reply comes from Ivdel that same night, requesting

Radiogram operator Igor Nevolin. Radiograms were the search teams' only connection to Ivdel. The device's misplaced battery was later found in a 2009 expedition. Second from left, Boris Slobtsov, third from left, Mikhail Sharavin, February 1959.

that a helicopter landing and campsite for roughly fifty people be arranged nearby. There are also strict orders that the items in the tent remain untouched. It is, of course, too late for that.

Word of the tent quickly spreads among the search groups, and the next day, multiple search teams arrive on the eastern slope to begin a more intensive search. Besides Slobtsov's and Nevolin's teams, there is a group headed by the Dyatlov group's hiking adviser, Yevgeny Maslennikov, and an Ivdel penitentiary unit led by a Captain Chernyshev. There are also Mansi volunteers, Sverdlovsk outdoorsmen and UPI students.

The newly arrived teams began examining the area in and around the tent in a way that Mikhail Sharavin later described as "chaotic" — a job, he says, that in hindsight should have been left to experienced investigators. But the lead prosecutor on the case,

View from the Dyatlov tent site. Photo taken by the rescue team,
February 28, 1959.

Drawing from Yevgeny Maslennikov's diary included in the
criminal case files: "Position of hollow and azimuth directions
to landmarks (height 1023, brook and outlier rock at the pass)
from Dyatlov tent."

Vasily Tempalov, has not yet arrived, and the searchers see no point
in wasting time with procedural formalities. In their eagerness to
find the hikers alive, searchers pick over the tent and its contents
for clues. Policemen with search dogs come, led by Lieutenant
Nikolay Moiseyev.

Unfortunately, there are no discernible tracks in the surrounding snow for the dog teams to follow. This is presumably due to
the slope's incline and the wind having swept away any traces of
footsteps. But if there had been evidence of the hikers' prints, the
teams of men now swarming the tent have certainly obliterated them.
Farther down the slope, however, where the land levels out, one of
the teams picks up impressions in the hardened snowpack. About
20 yards away from the tent there are multiple sets of footprints
that have remained preserved. Some of the prints are large. Others
are smaller and less distinct, as if the person who left them had not
been wearing shoes. The investigators count nine sets of prints,
extending for nearly half a mile toward the river valley. The tracks
are split into two parallel paths, continuing toward the valley before
merging again. The searchers follow this footpath until they hit a
patch of freshly fallen snow, at which point the prints disappear.
But the searchers continue on, hoping to pick up the trail again.

Meanwhile, about a mile away in the Lozva River valley, Mikhail
Sharavin and another member of Slobtsov's group, Yuri Koptelov,
are scouting an area suitable for camp. With the growing number of
searchers, they'll need a place to sleep for the night and a central
base where they can store equipment and send radiograms back to
Ivdel. Scouting out the evening's campsite is not the most thrilling task, but it's an order from Ivdel, and Sharavin doesn't argue.

Around midday, the young men come across a spot that doesn't
seem quite right. Beneath a large cedar tree, they notice charred
cedar boughs partially buried by snow. As they draw closer, they
find what looks like traces of a fire pit. The haphazard nature of the
pit tells them this was not a proper campsite. Nor does it appear to

Footprints made by one of the nine hikers,, February 1959.

be the remains of a Mansi fire, as the Mansi tended to stick close to the woods and river to set their winter fur traps.

Just north of the pit, one of the men points to something sticking out of the snow. As they draw closer, they see that it is a human knee.

SHARAVIN AND KOPTELOV LEAVE THE SITE UNDISTURBED and head back to camp to alert the others. A group including Yevgeny Maslennikov is dispatched to the cedar tree; and, when the snow is excavated from around the exposed knee, they find not one body, but two, lying side by side, both men. They are not wearing jackets, or, for that matter, pants. One has on a checkered shirt and a pair of swim trunks under long underwear. Only the right leg of the underwear remains, with the other leg torn away. His feet are bare,

A piece of clothing
found near the cedar
tree, February 1959.

with snow wedged between his toes. The other body is slightly more
covered, in an undershirt, a checkered shirt, long underwear, briefs
and socks. But the clothes on both bodies are brutally shredded, with
pieces apparently missing, leaving much of their discolored skin
exposed. One lies facedown in the snow, his arms folded under his
head like a pillow. There are broken cedar branches lying beneath
him. The other lies on his back, his face turned upward. His mouth
and eyes have been gotten at by an animal, probably a bird.

Despite the damage to his face, Sharavin and Koptelov are able
to recognize the upturned hiker as Georgy Krivonishchenko. The
body lying face down is his classmate, Yuri Doroshenko.

★

11

2012

MY FIRST INTERVIEW WITH YURI YUDIN HAD BEEN predictably stiff, but by our second meeting, he was relaxing into my company and joking about my fascination with the case. Like Kuntsevich, Yudin was perplexed by the idea of an American traveling to Russia to solve a mystery that by all appearances had nothing to do with him. "Do you not have mysteries in your own country?" he asked again, teasing this time.

As we sat down and I started the tape recorder, Yudin pulled out a yellowed songbook he used to take with him on hiking trips. Because there were few public radio stations broadcasting music in the '50s, he and his friends often had to make their own music. It was the beginning of what he called "an era of the bards," in which lyrics about love, nature and politics—accompanied by mandolin or guitar—became popular among Russia's youth. Bard songs, much like folk music in America, had spontaneously sprung up outside of the establishment. For those who wished to avoid reprisals from the Soviet government, these songs had to be memorized, as any recordings could serve as evidence against them. "We would be sitting on the train, and maybe one hundred students would be singing songs," Yudin said. "Sometimes they were very antigovernment, but no one worried about it."

On shorter trips, Yudin and his friends might take along a portable record player, and at night in the tent, they would play bard, jazz and classical music. Many of their records were etched on a kind of vinyl called *roentgenizdat* or "bone records," which were illegal. During World War II, rationing in Russia had made vinyl prohibitively expensive, and cheap X-ray film became the bootleg music industry's substitute. After purchasing a used X-ray plate for a ruble or two from a medical facility, music lovers could cut the plate into a disk with scissors or a knife before having it etched with their favorite tunes. Students studying engineering, I was told, particularly excelled in this bootlegging process.

But even a thawed Khrushchev regime had its standards to uphold, and in 1959 the government began a crackdown on this illicit music market. One government tactic was to flood record shops with unplayable records, many intended to damage record players. Some of these records included threatening vocals placed in the middle of a recording, which screamed at the unsuspecting listener, "You like rock and roll? Fuck you, anti-Soviet slime!" Eventually the use of bone records declined as replacement technologies, such as magnetic reel-to-reel tape, took over. But until then, bone-record makers were hunted down and sent to the Gulags. Particularly offensive to the Soviet government were bootleggers who reproduced American jazz records, music Stalin had declared a "threat to civilization."

Despite the capricious brutality of the Soviet government, Yudin remembers those times fondly. "We were poor, but we could live well because everything was cheap. The government helped us. They gave us money. And when it came to our hiking expeditions, they gave us money as well. . . . Now, under the Putin government, we are plankton. Now money is the authority. Money buys you freedom. I'm spitting on Yeltsin!" What Yudin said next sounded not only strange to my Western ears, but also surprising given his impoverished upbringing under Stalinist rule: "After Stalin's death, everybody cried, everybody was sad. . . . I think that Stalin did the right thing and that he was a great man."

As Yudin was telling me this, I noticed our translator shaking her head in vigorous disagreement. He didn't appear to notice her stern disapproval, and continued: "That said, I hate Lenin. He was not a good man. . . . Again, this is only my opinion." Before I could ask why he thought Stalin deserved such praise and not Lenin, Yudin abruptly segued into talk of the Dyatlov group's leader: "You could almost say that Igor was a totalitarian type of a leader at times. He decided everything."

This wasn't the first time I'd been told of Igor's dictatorial qualities. On my last trip I'd met with Aleksey Budrin, a friend of Igor's from UPI, who described how Igor had enforced peculiar rules on hiking trips, including the strictest personal hygiene. "We had to wash our feet every night, even though sometimes we didn't have a heater and maybe no hot water in winter," Budrin said. "You have to be quite a strong-willed man to make others do it because some people didn't want to. . . . It was quite unusual because no other hikers did anything like this, only Dyatlov."

There were more stories like this among the diary entries I'd had translated, including one from a 1957 summer excursion Igor had led into the Caucasus—a hiking party that included Zina and Kolya. En route, the group's westbound train passed through Stalingrad, inspiring Igor to pen a journal entry describing the still battle-scarred city. But beneath Igor's earnest descriptions of shell holes and Battle of Stalingrad memorials, Zina scribbled a teasing addendum. She described how Igor had intended to leave the group's backpacks on the train despite protests from the others that someone needed to stand guard. "At first Igor gave his decisive 'no,'" wrote Zina, "but when the guys assaulted him again, he stood and thought for a long time like some Napoleon, and then said quietly, 'Kolya and you, Zina, will stay.'"

As much as Igor preferred to control the course of the trips he led, the actual route of their final trip to Otorten Mountain had not, in fact, been his idea. "Originally it was the idea of some other hiking students," Yudin explained, "but they weren't good organizers and they failed to find people to go. And then our group decided to do it because Igor in particular had tremendous organizing skills."

In the years after the tragedy, one of the things that hurt Yudin most was how Igor and the others had been portrayed. Some of the published books, he felt, were merely searching for a lurid angle on the story: "Much has been made of the hikers' relationships with the opposite sex—that somehow arguments with the girls led to their deaths. This," he said, "is bullshit."

Then what did Yudin believe? In response to my questions, he made it clear that he didn't think the fate of his friends had anything to do with natural phenomena. "The number one possibility in my mind," he said, "is that it was people who came with guns because they were in an area they shouldn't have been in or they saw something they shouldn't have seen." He went on to say that the armed men had coerced the hikers into fabricating a scene to throw off investigators. The men forced them to walk into the forest half-naked, and to shred their own clothes before being left to die. "So they were forced to do it, to create this kind of madness."

The clue that most convinced Yudin that the hikers had been led by gunpoint was Lyuda's missing tongue. The reigning skeptic's interpretation was that nine bodies lying out in the open for days and weeks are going to attract animals, and that, not unlike the bird that damaged Georgy's face, the soft tissue of Lyuda's tongue had been a target for rodents. Yudin, however, doubted this explanation. "If it had been a mouse, it would have happened to everyone, to all the bodies." Instead, he believed someone had singled out Lyuda for punishment, possibly because she had been the most strong-willed and outspoken of the group. "Was it just an animal, or did she talk too much and that was a warning from government officials?"

In addition, a charm that Lyuda carried with her everywhere, a small stuffed toy in the shape of a hedgehog, had not been found on her body. "She always carried it with her, but it was missing." He pointed out that the chocolate the hikers had with them was also gone, with no evidence of the wrappers. Did someone whom the hikers encountered in the woods take these items, thinking that no one would notice? If so, who?

Later that night, as I reviewed the tape of our interview, I couldn't help but feel slightly deflated that Yudin stood squarely in the company of Dyatlov case conspiracists. Lyuda's toy was among the objects found at the campsite, and there was no evidence of her tongue being cut out, just missing. For all his connection to the tragedy, he was apparently no different from the many who suspected a government cover-up. In fact, his theory was nearly identical to the one related to me by Kuntsevich, who thought secret government case files would eventually prove him and others like him right.

Odder still had been Yudin's expression of his devotion not just to Stalin, but to Communist rule in general. How was Yudin able to reconcile a deep affection for the Soviet era, while carrying around an intense suspicion of its government? How could the same government that had provided for him and his family so well, who had given him a free education, be the same government responsible for, at best, whitewashing what happened the night of February 1—or, at worst, killing and torturing his closest friends? But Yudin's apparent love-hate relationship with strong rule was certainly not unique to him; one had only to look at his country's volatile history to see that this kind of ambivalence appeared to be stamped into the Russian genetic code.

Still, I was enjoying my days with Yudin and looking forward to having him beside me to provide commentary during our upcoming trip. But, as I would soon find out, my face time with the Dyatlov group's survivor would be limited. The next few days would bring discouraging news to the Kuntsevich house, as well as a surprise visitor from Moscow.

The Dyatlov hikers depart Vizhay for Sector 41, January 26, 1959.

★

12

THEY HAD BEEN EXPECTING NOTHING MORE THAN HUMBLE accommodations in Vizhay: just a roof over their heads and a floor on which to stretch out. But when Igor introduced himself and his companions to the director of the free workers' camp, the man took an instant liking to the young adventurers and insisted they spend the night at the camp's guesthouse. There they would be well taken care of and each provided with his or her own room. Yudin describes it as the most "posh" house in the settlement, a mansion in comparison with what they were used to. "It was very chic for those times," he says.

The instant they stepped over the threshold into their well-appointed lodgings, they were conscious of their grimy state. "The linens were spotless," Yudin remembers. "I was missing a pillowcase and a woman promptly found me a replacement." He adds, "The cleaning ladies, they were furious because they had to clean the whole place after we left."

After unloading their packs and spreading out in their luxurious digs, the hikers lit the wood-burning stove and started dinner. There were other tasks. Zina finished assembling her tarpaulin boot covers and Rustik wrote a postcard to his family. After dinner, there was talk of going into town. As chance would have it, the group's favorite movie, *Symphony in Gold*, was playing at the local cinema. The 1956 Austrian musical, which features an attractive cast ice skating its way through a snowy wonderland and effervescent musical numbers, was just then making its rounds in Soviet theaters. The hikers had seen *Symphony in Gold* multiple times and knew many of the songs by heart, even though the lyrics were in German. One particular number, "Dong Dingeldang," features an idyllic mountain landscape populated by a troop of young skiers buoyantly advancing through the snow. Apart from all the yodeling, and the comic arrival of an ice-skating bull, it's hard to imagine Igor and his friends not having seen themselves reflected in this scene of winter adventure and joyful song.

While the others were at the "cinema"—which was likely little more than a community projection room with folding chairs—the ever-sensible Kolevatov, with the help of Doroshenko, stayed behind to clear away the clutter from dinner. Referring to himself in the third person, Kolevatov noted somewhat bitterly in the group's diary:

> *Doroshenko and Kolevatov are left to do housework, while the others go to the cinema and return in "musical mood" after seeing Symphony in Gold.*

THE NEXT MORNING, THE TRAVELERS LEARNED THAT THE truck headed to Sector 41 wouldn't be leaving until that afternoon. This gave them ample time to pack and secure some breakfast. Georgy's diary notes:

> *We didn't cook in the morning, firewood is damp, and cooking took 6 hours in the evening. We went to the cafeteria for breakfast and had goulash a-la-cafeteria and tea.*

The goulash didn't present any particular reason for complaint, but the hikers were disappointed when their tea arrived unheated.

Igor, however, took the nuisance in stride. According to Georgy's diary, he quipped, "If the tea is cold, drink it outside and it will seem warmer."

After breakfast and packing, the morning's main task was to gather some final supplies in town and to get advice from the local forester. "In any settlement, the first visit was paid to foresters," Yudin explains, "because they knew the roads and could advise visitors on their route." Vizhay's resident forester was a man named Ivan Rempel. He was unusual among those in his profession in that he was part of a population known as Russified Germans, transplants from Germany who had embraced Russian culture and were fluent in the language.

Despite the forester's convincing assimilation, there was an aspect of his house that had retained the flavor of his home country, something Yudin noticed immediately upon entering. First, the house was exceedingly well kept. But most notably, Rempel had fashioned a section of his house in the likeness of a *Wunderkammer* or "wonder room"—what the English would call a cabinet of curiosities. The walls were covered in paintings, many of them done by Rempel himself. But most captivating to his visitors were shelves upon shelves of glass jars filled with miniature tableaux. Each jar featured a different shrunken landscape, and many were religious or seasonal in theme—motionless versions of the scenes Yudin and his friends had enjoyed at the cinema the night before. There were depictions of the Nativity, Christmas trees, winter vistas featuring children and sleighs and—the Slavic version of Santa Claus—Father Frost. While Igor and his friends were consulting with Rempel, Yudin couldn't keep his eyes from the diminutive figures suspended behind glass, and from the tiny Christ child lying in an equally tiny manger. To this day, Yudin can't understand how the forester managed to construct such tiny wonders. "How he got them in there, nobody could figure out."

While Yudin was enraptured by these fantasy snowscapes, the forester warned the rest of the hikers of the real winter conditions outside. After Igor expressed the group's intention to reach Otorten Mountain, the forester strongly advised against such a trip. "I expressed my opinion that it is dangerous to go over the Ural ridge in winter," Rempel later said, "as there are large ravines and pits where one can sink, and winds are so strong that people can be blown away." Rempel told the hikers that although he hadn't experienced these dangers firsthand, he had heard stories of locals making the mistake of similar trips.

But whatever argument the forester made, Igor insisted that they were looking for a challenge. "We are prepared, we're ready, we're not afraid," Yudin remembers Igor saying. "The level of preparation for the campaign of the Dyatlov group was much better than that assumed by local residents."

Even if Igor had believed that significant danger lay ahead, as the forester was insisting, he wouldn't have let that discourage his group. Igor was "a fan of extremely dangerous situations—an addict," Yudin says. "He was deliberately finding and choosing the most dangerous situations and overcoming them." Perhaps, then, the forester's warning had the opposite effect to the one intended: It only convinced Igor that he and his friends were on the right path. After Igor copied down one of Rempel's maps, which was more detailed than the one they were carrying, the friends thanked the forester, cast a last glance at the miniature curios and went on their way.

It was around this time that Yudin began to have serious doubts about continuing into the mountains. It had nothing to do with the forester's warnings and everything to do with the increasing pain shooting through his back and legs. Yudin informed the group of his discomfort—stated merely as fact, not as a complaint—but also said he fully intended to push ahead to Sector 41.

That afternoon, the ten bundled friends piled into the bed of a woodcutters' truck, one primarily used for shuttling workers to and from the camps. As Yudin would discover during the three-hour truck ride, this form of transportation was not designed for someone combating rheumatism. Aside from the extreme cold, every bump and irregularity in the road seemed to magnify his pain. He could do little about the roughness, but he resorted to unfurling the group's tent and pulling it over himself like a blanket to keep warm. Georgy noted how the friends tried to make the best of an uncomfortable journey:

> Got pretty cold, as we were riding in the back of a GAZ-63. We were singing all the way, discussing various issues, from love and friendship to cancer diseases and treatment.

"The wind was blowing in our faces," Yudin remembers. "The temperature was very low and my clothes were very thin." Yudin would later catch cold because of this ride, but then a cold was trivial as compared with his lifelong struggles with illness. "It's a Russian way of thinking. When we are ill, we think, OK, I'm not going to the doctor. I'm not going to lie about it either, but maybe it'll go away."

Though he had told his friends that he intended to push onward, Yudin knew he wouldn't be able to bear such pain once they were deep in the Urals. There was only so much relief the medicine in his pack could provide. As the truck rattled its way to Sector 41, and Yudin's bones rattled along with it, he was keenly aware that at some point there would be no turning back. He would have to make a decision soon.

Stepan Kurikov, head of the Mansi search team, February 1959.

★

13

STEPAN KURIKOV TRUDGES THROUGH A SMALL RAVINE, A lead in his hand and a police dog at the other end of it. Kurikov has come to the search by way of Suyevatpaul, a Mansi village at the Anchucha tributary, where he is one of the respected tribal elders. He is also one of few Mansi tribesmen who has joined the search, and though he is well into his fifties, he is a tireless member of the team. Trailing behind him is Vladislav Karelin, a medical engineering employee and a Grade-II hiker. Karelin was a member of the same hiking group that stopped for tea at the Mansi village of Bahtiyarova earlier in the month—a visit that initially threw off searchers after they confused Karelin's party with Dyatlov's.

As the two weave through the dark claws of dormant birches, Kurikov senses that his dog is anxious, in the way that police dogs get right before they find something. It is late afternoon and Kurikov and Karelin are only a few hundred yards from where the bodies of Yuri Doroshenko and Georgy Krivonishchenko were found several hours earlier. It's strange that Kurikov should find himself here again, in the same spot that he and another Mansi volunteer had combed just days before with no success. If not for the two searchers stumbling upon the bodies earlier that morning, the teams would still be swarming the eastern slope. But now the focus has shifted to the valley, almost a mile from the Dyatlov group's tent.

The German shepherd tugs at its lead, pulling Kurikov over the powdery snow in the direction of a young birch, whose shoots erupt from the ground at unnatural angles, as if coerced by gravity or wind. The Mansi man watches as the dog sniffs around the sapling, leaving behind a mess of paw prints. As the shepherd grows increasingly anxious, Kurikov calls to his companion. There can be no doubt there is something here, and the men drop to their knees and begin to dig. With gloved hands, they toss the snow behind them in clumps. But they don't have to dig far because just inches beneath the surface, they hit something hard. They find a patch of dark cloth, and after more snow is cleared away, they can make out the shape of a joint covered in wool—an elbow.

Like a pair of archaeologists, the men continue to carve away the snow, until something human emerges. First an arm, then hands, and another arm, until it becomes clear that the arms are held across the chest in what appears to be a defensive gesture. But in fact, the arms are clutching the birch, pulling its spindly trunk downward, giving the tree its awkward angle. As the men unearth more of the body, they observe that this hiker is dressed more warmly than Doroshenko and Krivonishchenko had been, though not by much. This man wears a sweater pulled over a checkered shirt, plus a fur vest and ski trousers. Like his companions, he is without hat or gloves. He is also shoeless, with only a pair of mismatched socks pulled over painfully curled feet. On his left wrist is a Zvezda watch—a popular brand manufactured north of Moscow in Uglich. The watch is stopped at 5:31. The position of the body, as it clings to the birch, is one of suspended struggle, as if the victim had been fighting against the elements until his last breath.

Kurikov has never met any of the Dyatlov hikers and is hardly in a position to identify the body. But Karelin not only knows this man, he helped secure maps for his group's trip to Otorten

Igor Dyatlov's partially buried body, February 27, 1959.

Mountain. As Karelin wipes the encrusted snow from the rigid, upturned face, he is confronted with the unmistakable features of the hiking party's leader, Igor Dyatlov.

AFTER NEWS OF THE BODY IS DELIVERED BACK TO CAMP, searchers begin to fan out from the birch. Lieutenant Nikolay Moiseyev, who leads the second police dog of the company, heads from the tree back in the direction of the hikers' tent. Several hundred yards from the birch, as the land slopes upward from the valley, his dog, Alma, starts to pace back and forth over a smooth patch of snow. Moiseyev has made a career of interpreting canine behavior. Back at his precinct in Sverdlovsk, he is primarily known for two things: telling good stories and training police dogs. He works mostly with German shepherds, but he has also trained Eastern-European shepherds, a military breed developed in the 1930s by crossing German shepherds with Russian breeds. For years, he has been preparing these animals to sniff out contraband and missing persons, yet he can't help but feel his heart sink when his efforts pay off at a moment like this, above several feet of snow.

Alma stops and begins to dig. Moiseyev drops to his knees to join her, their efforts soon revealing a figure just beneath the surface. It is clear from the smaller stature that this is a woman. She lies on her right side, face down, arms twisted beneath her. Her pretty face is dark with dried blood, and her right leg is bent, as if she had been in midclimb before collapsing. Unlike the other bodies, however, she is the first to be dressed somewhat sensibly for the climate. She wears a hat, ski jacket and ski pants. Yet, like the others, she is mysteriously without shoes. Her feet are covered only in socks.

Because he does not know her, Moiseyev is unable to name the victim on the spot, but a radiogram sent back to Ivdel later that day would identify the young woman's body as Zina Kolmogorova.

THAT SAME DAY, WHILE MOISEYEV AND HIS MEN ARE searching the valley, Yevgeny Maslennikov—the man who advised Dyatlov and his friends before their trip—is appointed head of the entire search operation. It is a post for which he is well qualified. Maslennikov is not only head of the hiking club at the metal plant where he works, he is one of the few in Sverdlovsk who can boast a Master of Sport certification. And because he knew all of the missing hikers personally—with the exception of Zolotaryov—he is one of the few searchers who is able to identify the bodies on the spot.

Once bodies start turning up—and in the continued absence of the lead prosecutor—Maslennikov takes a turn at investigator and begins to suggest theories as to what might have happened to his young friends. His radiograms back to Ivdel sketch out an early theory that the hikers were swept down the slope by gale-force winds:

```
WE DIDN'T HAVE TIME TO EXAMINE TENT
PROBABLY THEY WERE BURIED UNDER HEAVY SNOW
THE TENT GOT TORN PEOPLE STOOD UP WERE SWEPT AWAY
    DOWNHILL BY WIND.
```

This echoed a radiogram sent from camp earlier in the day from other members of the search team:

```
IN 16 HOURS 4 BODIES FOUND IN DIFFERENT PLACES,
AND THEY ARE SCARCELY DRESSED AND BAREFOOT,
WHICH LEADS US TO BELIEVE THEY WERE SWEPT BY
A STORM.
```

Yet even this early theory, which seemed to make perfect sense to the people on the ground, wasn't adding up for those back in Ivdel. A committee secretary by the name of Zaostrovsky inquired:

```
WHY WERE THINGS LEFT IN THE TENT IF PEOPLE WERE
SWEPT AWAY BY WIND?
```

More specifically, why would the tent—including all its contents and support posts—be left intact when the hikers had been swept away so forcefully? This seemingly innocuous question posed by radiogram would turn out to be one of the most baffling questions of the case, one that would ceaselessly plague investigators.

Search team gathers at Boot Rock, February 1959.

FEBRUARY 27 WAS AN EVENTFUL DAY FOR THE SEARCHERS, but by the end of it, five hikers are still unaccounted for. The next day, having exhausted the area near the birch and cedar trees, Maslennikov has his teams focus on the trail of footprints leading downhill from the tent—a path that had turned up nothing the previous day. Surprisingly, the search dogs that were so useful the day before, are now encountering difficulty. In a radiogram, Maslennikov calls Moiseyev's dogs "useless" in deep snow. To tackle the snow problem, Moiseyev outfits his searchers with steel avalanche probes—instruments that, incidentally, had been manufactured at the very metal plant in which Maslennikov works. Probing snow is more difficult than it sounds; some patches of snow are so dense that it requires a strenuous effort to shove the probe all the way to the permafrost. A single searcher

could make 10,000 picks in the snow per day, covering an area of up to 30,000 yards, yet still turn up nothing.

The four bodies that were previously found have been wrapped in tarpaulin and stored about a mile from Holatchahl mountain under a large, boot-shaped rock, dubbed "Boot Rock." Meanwhile, Maslennikov continues to puzzle over the evidence, articulating his confusion in another radiogram to Ivdel:

```
WHY THE WHOLE GROUP LEFT TENT HALF-DRESSED, WE
  DON'T KNOW YET.
ABSOLUTELY NO NOTION.
```

That same day, a helicopter lands near search headquarters, and the lead prosecutor from Ivdel emerges. Vasily Tempalov, the man with zero experience on such cases, has arrived at last. He gets to work on catching himself up on the day's events, cataloguing the tent's contents, and making his official report. He notes the following facts:

```
The tent was set on the slope at a height of
  1,079 meters.
An even spot was made under the tent, with skis
  laid at the bottom.
The tent was covered with snow.
The entrance was partly open, with sheet cur-
  tains sticking out.
Urine traces were found where someone had been
  "taking a leak."
When the tent was dug out, a tear in the tent
  on the slope-facing side close to the entrance
  was found, with a fur jacket sticking out of
  the hole.
```

```
The descent-facing side was torn to pieces.
A pair of bound skis was lying in front of the
    tent entrance.
Arrangement of things inside the tent are
    catalogued.
```

Many of these items had been observed by the men who had discovered the tent two days ago. There is one peculiarity, however, that no one had previously noticed: a series of rips in the canvas, at the back of the tent to the north. But then, in an already threadbare structure, a few rips don't seem to hold tremendous significance. In fact, it is regarded as so insignificant that no one could later remember who made the discovery.

AT THE DAY'S END, MASLENNIKOV NOTES THAT NO OTHER bodies were found. He also notes in a radiogram the items that Tempalov had taken from the site:

```
THE PROSECUTOR TOOK ALL OF THE GROUP'S DOCUMENTS
    EXCEPT FOR SKETCHES AND PERSONAL NOTEBOOKS,
    INCLUDING 3 COPIES OF THE ROUTE SCHEDULE. . . .
```

But, as it happened, it mattered little what Prosecutor Tempalov did that day. Once Tempalov returned to Ivdel, he wouldn't get a chance even to initiate his case; and, within two days' time, his services would no longer be required. In fact, after the first bodies had been found the day before, higher-ups in the regional prosecutor's office were already arranging to have Tempalov replaced by a more powerful prosecutor. By March 1, they would settle on Lev Ivanov, a man who would come to personify the Dyatlov case

Lev Ivanov, n.d.

for decades to come. Ivanov liked to tell people that his personal motto for success was "I am honest, not corrupt, and I sleep well." By the end of the case, however, Ivanov would betray his motto on at least two of these counts.

★

14

KUNTSEVICH'S BASEMENT APARTMENT HAD BECOME A
kind of war room for our trip preparations. Each morning after
breakfast, I descended the cement stairs to spend some time with
Yuri Yudin, and each day the living room grew smaller as it filled
with gear for our trip. As our departure date drew near, Yudin gave
me some disappointing news. Through our translator, he informed
me that he wouldn't be making the trip to the mountains, though
he declined to give me a specific reason. I was disheartened that the
Dyatlov group's only survivor wouldn't be at my side as we retraced
his own footsteps over half a century later. I hadn't expected Yudin
to go all the way to Dyatlov Pass, but I had hoped he would join us
for at least part of the expedition. His decision shouldn't have come
as too much of a surprise. If Yudin hadn't been able to complete
the trip in the winter of 1959 at the age of twenty-one, it seemed
a stretch to expect him to attempt the same trip at seventy-four.
(He had, however, returned to the area in the summer of 1963 to
partake in a ceremony to honor his fallen friends.)

On the morning two days before we were to leave, I told
Kuntsevich that I'd be in the war room and made my way downstairs. I opened the door to find a man in his mid-sixties, who was
not Yudin, sitting on the couch. It took me several seconds before
I could place him: It was my "attorney" from Moscow. After I got
over my initial surprise, Vladimir Borzenkov and I greeted each

other with a sturdy handshake. He had clearly traveled a great distance to be here—if not by plane, then a sixteen-hour train ride from Moscow. By all appearances, this was not a casual visit.

Thirty minutes later, our translator, Olga Taranenko, arrived—the same young woman who had made her feelings about Stalin abundantly clear a few days before. Taranenko had been born and raised in Yekaterinburg, though she had never heard of the Dyatlov incident until this job. As her interest in the case grew, she asked to accompany us on the journey as our interpreter. But Kuntsevich had declined, saying he did not feel it would be safe to bring a young woman into the mountains.

Now that Borzenkov and I could at last communicate, the first thing I learned was that he would be accompanying Kuntsevich and me on our trip. Then, like an excited kid, Borzenkov proudly revealed his hiking gear piled behind a chair. He pulled out a multicolor, nylon snowsuit from his pack and held it up for my admiration. Patched together like a frenetic quilt—half Piet Mondrian, half Russian superhero—it was unlike any snowsuit I have seen. He pulled out the matching accessories—a hood, backpack and nylon gloves—and explained that he'd designed the suit himself, in conjunction with the Sports Federation of the USSR. Along with three similar jackets and two pairs of trousers, his suits had survived fifty ski trips and search and rescue expeditions, including sojourns to the Kola Peninsula, the Polar Urals and the Arctic. He then joked that all the nations of the world were represented in this suit, making him a walking United Nations.

I pointed to the baby-blue aviation patch on the suit's left arm, which prompted Borzenkov to elaborate on his background and education. He was not an attorney at all. He was a third-generation Muscovite who had earned the patch from the Moscow State University of Aeronautics, formerly known as the Moscow Aviation Institute. There, he took three higher education degrees: one in aviation engineering, another in applied mathematics and a third—the equivalent of a PhD—in safety-and-rescue equipment engineering for aviation and space systems. After earning his engineering degrees, Borzenkov had joined the 1982 scientific team behind the first official Soviet expedition to the summit of Mount Everest. In addition to designing climate-specific suits for the twenty-six-man team, he also created a special oxygen mask mechanism that, after its success on the Everest expedition, was used in the Soviet space program.

"Our mountaineers chose an extremely difficult and untrodden route at the southwest side of Everest," he told me. "The expedition had two night ascents never made by anyone else. What was most rewarding for me and everyone involved in designing oxygen equipment for that expedition was that for the first time in Russian history, our mountaineers didn't experience a single failure of oxygen masks."

When I asked him how he had come to know so much about the Dyatlov expedition, he told me that in the late '70s his experience as a hiking consultant led to a position as vice president of the Federation of Student Tourism for the fifteen Soviet republics. In his new position, he familiarized himself with hiking accidents and tragedies that had involved university students. "It was purely administrative and methodological work," he explained. "I was personally responsible for safety issues and was often inspecting hiking regions frequented during student vacations. We kept watch there as a rescue team, equipped to provide first aid."

His mood seemed to darken when I asked him about rescues he'd been involved in. His first search and rescue mission, he told me, had been in 1971 to the Kola Peninsula in northwest Russia. "Schoolchildren from Polyarnye Zori town were on a ski tour in the Khibiny Mountains, and one boy lagged behind. The group was large, and they hurried to catch a train. The leader only discovered the boy was missing on the train. The next day, a rescue team of three people, including me, went to look for the boy. We were volunteers because there was no professional rescue agency yet. I had just returned from a ski trip and was in Kirovsk town. . . . The weather was very bad, with strong winds up to 95 miles per hour and frost around −20°C [−3°F]. We could not go through one pass on the route because it was a narrow cleft, and wind would simply blow us out from its entrance. The team moving to meet us from the other end of the route had the same problem. We searched through all nooks of the route assigned to us. Later, we found the boy, after the weather improved, right in that cleft where we couldn't pass. Unfortunately, we could not help him. He had frozen on the first day. It was my first expedition, and it ended badly, so many details stayed in my memory for a long time, haunting me."

It was in 1978, while Borzenkov was reviewing previous hiking accidents, that he came upon information about the incident at Dyatlov Pass. But it wasn't until 1984, while attending a conference on aviation and space ergonomics, that he met some of the volunteers who had taken part in the search efforts. From then on, he could not shake the case from his mind.

As we spent more time together, it became clear that Borzenkov was not a Dyatlov case conspiracist, but rather was holding out for a scientific explanation. Kuntsevich, by contrast, was a man who relied on his gut instinct, even if his interpretations of the facts were sometimes tinged with hyperbole. The two men, however, had been friends since the '60s, brethren of the last Soviet generation, and weren't afraid to engage in a heated debate. Both were striving to finally solve the case and help the still-grieving families of the hikers find solace.

★

I KNEW NOTHING OF PACKING FOR A TRIP OF THIS magnitude. At least, this was the conclusion I came to as my Russian friends schooled me in the ways of winter mountaineering.

First, Kuntsevich told me that I would need the following items on my person at all times: a pocketknife, two lighters and one box of matches. Preferably, the matches should be sewn into my clothes. I was then taught how to arrange my clothes in the order of usage—which, I realized, meant that I was supposed to schedule my daily wardrobe ahead of time. Once I had my clothing timeline sorted out, I was instructed to roll each article as compactly as possible to save space. Kuntsevich then loaded me up with my share of pots, pans and other odds and ends. Borzenkov informed me that the lighter items belonged at the bottom of the backpack, while the heavier items—completely counter to my intuition— were to be placed at the top near my head. I stopped myself from protesting, reminding myself that the man knew a little something about physics.

At some point, Borzenkov and I became engaged in a side-by-side comparison of our respective gear, a contest that seemed to carry with it a certain Cold War one-upmanship. If I had been harboring any lingering feelings of superiority about my fancy outerwear or highfalutin boots, Borzenkov quickly shot me down with a display of his impressive Russian headlamp—which, he pointed out, was of a more solid construction than my made-in-the-USA equivalent. More embarrassing were the shell pants I had thought such a wise purchase several months ago, which ended up not fitting around my fancy Arctic-model "elephant boots," as Kuntsevich dubbed them. The miscalculation would have me running around last-minute to find Russian-made snow pants fit for the journey.

As we counted down the days to our departure, Kuntsevich, Borzenkov and I were already kidding around with friendly ease— through Taranenko's translations. Our banter held the familiar lightness of tone that tends to happen in the face of a serious task. It reminded me of the gaiety of dorm room 531 on January 23, 1959, as Igor and the others packed for their last adventure together. As I glanced at Yudin, I wondered if he was thinking of that night as he observed our preparations.

Yudin hovered around us, stopping every once in a while to make private notes on scraps of paper. Whether these notes were vital, or Yudin simply wished to look busy, I wasn't sure. Occasionally, he'd chime in to the conversation, but most of the time he was a silent presence in the room, content to observe the activity around him. Tragedy couldn't have been far from his mind, as his constant refrain in the days leading up to our expedition was, "I am praying for your safety."

ON THE AFTERNOON OF THE DAY BEFORE OUR DEPARTURE, Kuntsevich's wife pulled me and the translator into the kitchen. What I assumed was another of Olga's afternoon tea breaks or a surprise serving of *salo*—a delicacy made from cured pig fat—turned out to be a private talk out of earshot of the others. She told me in a near whisper that her husband was very worried for my safety, so much so that he was considering canceling the trip entirely. Her concern touched me, but I assured her—while ignoring my own doubts—that everything would be fine, I was certain of it.

When I rejoined the others, Kuntsevich was soberly discussing the weather forecast, which he pointed out was particularly difficult to predict in the region from Ivdel to the mountains. He explained that we would have to bypass the village of Vizhay, where the hikers had stayed for one night. A wildfire had struck the village in the summer of 2010, consuming thirty-four buildings and resulting in the entire community's evacuation to Ivdel. Similarly, Sector 41 no longer existed, as such woodcutting settlements had typically been razed after five years of use. We would, however, be staying in Ushma, a Mansi village located along the Lozva River, five miles downstream from where the hikers had spent the night in Sector 41. Lacking the modern conveniences of running water and electricity, Ushma was the closest we could come to spending the night as the hikers had done.

Kuntsevich's worry was that in the 45 miles between Ushma and Dyatlov Pass, a region known for its hurricane-force winds, weather prediction was utterly useless. The temperate forecasts were saying minus twenty-five degrees Fahrenheit, the same estimated temperature the hikers had experienced on their last night together. But even that prediction could change for the worse.

Having never experienced these kinds of brutal temperatures firsthand, I started to get a little nervous and, amid all the talk of worst-case scenarios, I had to suppress my own feelings of escalating dread. My talk in the kitchen with Olga had only made me more aware of the concern I saw on Kuntsevich's face whenever he looked in my direction. If the stoic Russians were this nervous about our journey into the northern Ural Mountains, how was I supposed to feel?

Our morning call time was seven o'clock, and as I prepared for bed, I gave myself a mental pep talk. This hike was exactly what I was supposed to be doing, I told myself. It was what I had been wanting for several years. Before I could disappear into my room for the night, Borzenkov pulled me aside with one last bit of mountaineering wisdom, delivered in halting English. I was expecting another warning—a *remember to*, or *never*, or *always*—but instead he told me not to bother packing a toothbrush. He didn't tell me why, but he said it with such gravity, that for a second I believed it to be sage advice. In the end, I made sure that my toothbrush was easily accessible in the side pocket of my pack. My new friend, after all, was missing a significant number of his teeth.

The last bit of business before bed was to call my family. First, I called my girlfriend on Skype, in what turned into a teary half-hour exchange, at the end of which I promised her that I'd return home safely. Even more poignant was my son's puzzled look as he stared at the computer screen at a face he was having trouble placing, but one that his mother kept referring to as "Papa." His lack of recognition cut my heart in half. I had only been gone a couple of weeks, but to a one-year-old, that was an eternity.

The last call was to my mother, whose refrain throughout this quest of mine had been: "Why are you doing this?" When my mother asked me again, "Why are you doing this?" I didn't have a satisfying answer for her. I told her not to worry and that I'd be home soon.

Zinaida "Zina" Kolmogorova in Sector 41 wearing the
boot covers she made in Vizhay, January 27, 1959.

★

15

THE WOODCUTTERS LIVING IN SECTOR 41 HAD LIKELY NOT seen a woman in months, and when the truck bearing the ten hikers came into view, the two women aboard must have sent a collective tremor through the laborers' hearts. It was about an hour before sunset, and, as the hikers climbed out of the truck to greet their hosts, there was still enough light for the strangers to see each other clearly. The woodcutters were bundled in the standard outerwear of the region: trapper's cap and *telogreika*—a quilted cotton jacket originally designed for the Red Army. The men had young, unlined faces, and the hikers recognized that they were not much older than themselves. Among those who greeted them, there was one proud man who stood out from the rest. He had dark, disheveled hair and a full red beard. He introduced himself as Yevgeny Venediktov, though Georgy noted he had a fitting nickname.

> *We were talking to local workers about all kinds of things for a rather long time, and one red-bearded worker stayed in memory, his fellows called him "Boroda."*

Boroda (the Russian word for "beard") considered himself the spokesman of the group, and he took immediate charge in finding rooms for their guests. Aside from a series of pine log cabins that served as dorms for the workers, there was little to see at Sector 41. The settlement was like many of its kind in the region—a collection of roughly fifty men sent out on long-term contracts to harvest, chop and haul wood from the surrounding forests. The life of a woodcutter was an isolated one, and it took men away from their families for extended portions of the year. But then, for Soviets who lacked a formal education, manual labor was often their best option. Perhaps it was at moments such as these that the ten hikers felt lucky to have been awarded a place at the university; even under Khrushchev, there were many young people whose opportunities were startlingly limited.

While the woodcutters were enlivened by the appearance of unexpected guests, the hikers were simply relieved their windblown ride was at an end. There was dinner and sleep to look forward to, and, for Yuri Yudin, there was the temporary reprieve from the painful jostle of travel. The ten friends unloaded their packs from the truck. After displacing some of his fellow workers, Boroda managed to free up a separate room for their female guests. Lyuda and Zina appreciated the gesture, but as it happened, there would be little time for sleep that night.

The woodcutters made bread for their visitors, and after dinner, everyone gathered around the wood-burning stove for warmth. The cabin offered none of the comforts of the Vizhay guesthouse. The furniture was Spartan, and patches of swamp moss wedged between the logs were the only thing keeping out the bitter draft. But the cabin was luxurious compared with the accommodations that lay ahead for the hikers, and they were surely grateful for the warm reception and company. In fact, the students from the city found that they had more in common with these rural laborers than they might have guessed. It was true that the woodcutters had the wiry bodies of men who made their living from the land, but they also had the minds of self-taught intellectuals and the hearts of poets. Of all the men, the hikers

Sector 41 woodcutters. Far left, Yevgeny "Boroda" Venediktov,
January 27, 1959.

The Dyatlov hikers in their Sector 41 quarters. Igor Dyatlov
(middle) and Nikolay "Kolya" Thibault-Brignoles (right, wearing
hat). Yuri "Georgy" Krivonishchenko's mandolin hangs on the
wall behind them, January 27, 1959.

found Boroda to be the most like-minded. Not only could he recite poetry as if he were reading it from the pages of a book, but he also held an easy sway over the entire group. "He was clearly the smartest," Yudin recalls, "and he had immense authority among the guys." Boroda also had a striking personal style for a man who spent most of his life in the woods. His reluctance to shave may well have arisen from convenience, but when paired with his smart blazer and Cossack-style breeches, Boroda's generous facial hair lent him a surprising air of sophistication. It was as if he were making a conscious fashion statement, even if out here in the Russian wood there were few to admire it.

Over multiple cups of black tea, which was in plentiful supply from China during that time, Boroda and his crew recited their favorite poems for their guests. "Even though they worked as forest cutters, they knew Yesenin and his poems," Yudin remembers. "So that shows that they were smart, not just working class." Sergei Yesenin was a lyrical poet of the early twentieth century, one of the most celebrated in Russia. He had been an early supporter of the Bolshevik Revolution, but his later criticism of the government compelled Stalin to ban his work—a ban that had remained in place through Khrushchev's regime. Yesenin had also been plagued by mental illness, and at the age of thirty hanged himself. But just before ending his life, he wrote what would become one of his most famous poems:

Good-bye, my friend, good-bye
My love, you are in my heart.
It was preordained we should part
And be reunited by and by.
Good-bye: no handshake to endure.
Let's have no sadness—furrowed brow.
There's nothing new in dying now
Though living is no newer.

Poetry lovers living in the Soviet Union would have had to memorize poems such as this one, as it was difficult to find Yesenin's work in print. "You couldn't read his books," Yudin explains. "They were forbidden. You couldn't buy them anywhere. . . . But even though he was forbidden—as were many other poets and writers—somehow we managed to have conversations about him."

As often happens, talk of poetry among young people turns to talk of love and relationships. And that night the two women steered the conversation toward romance. Yudin remembers that the two women were fond of this type of talk, and they had often brought up the subject back at the UPI dorms. "So every day since we left Yekaterinburg they were talking about love. They were trying to express something and to get to know something from the guys."

Only a couple of days earlier, Yudin had noted as much in the group diary: "Dispute about love provoked by Z. Kolmogorova." Zina evidently wasn't finished with the dispute, and her male hosts provided a fresh perspective on the subject. But Zina's motives, as well as Lyuda's, were entirely innocent, Yudin says. Most members of the group, including both women, were virgins. "Life was different in those times, and the atmosphere was different. Nobody would understand that now. Everything was romantic, but the romance meant something different."

Yudin admits that the male members of the hiking group—Igor, Georgy and Doroshenko, in particular—had crushes on Zina, but he says there was shame attached to expressing interest in one person. "Of course, we had some romantic feelings toward each other, but nobody said anything because you couldn't pay attention to one girl. It wouldn't be the Soviet style of doing things." Of the talk that night at Sector 41, Yudin says, "Of course we had affections toward each other, but the talks were about love in general, not in particular. . . . What is love? What is romance? Who's the perfect girl, the perfect type of girl?"

The friends may have preferred to speak of their feelings in universal terms, but they didn't hesitate to sing and dance with each other, celebrating the romance of being young, together and, perhaps, secretly in love. The musical Rustik took a turn on Georgy's mandolin, while one of the woodcutters produced a guitar. Among the many songs of the evening was "Snow" by the Russian poet and adventurer Alexander Gorodnitsky, whose songs were popular among young travelers.

Silently slowly sliding snow,
Crackling twigs in the sputtering fire,
Everyone's still asleep but I—
What's on my mind?

It's snowing snow, snowing snow,
Priming the tent's canvas in white
Our short stay overnight
Is almost over.

It's snowing snow, snowing snow,
Painting the tundra around us white;
Making the frozen rivers alight,
Snowing snow.

All this celebrating was, of course, conducted without consuming alcohol—at least for the hikers. "Nobody drank, among the tourists, nobody," Yudin insists, though he admits that he and his friends made exceptions on special occasions. On one particular New Year's Eve, a group of roughly one hundred students went camping, bringing two bottles of champagne to go around. "Everybody had a spoonful of champagne and that's it. But we were dancing and singing all night, because we didn't need alcohol to have fun."

And so, without the aid of beer, wine, or moonshine, the students laughed with their hosts, stomped on the wooden floorboards and generally amused themselves until there were only a few hours of remaining darkness. Only then did they retire to their rooms and fall into a much-needed sleep. The group had a difficult day of travel ahead of them. They were now finished with motorized transportation; it was time to ready their skis and test their physical abilities in the wild.

Yuri Yudin did not sleep soundly that night. He awoke from his bed on the floor to an even worse pain than he had experienced the day before. Yet he was determined to push ahead. His stubbornness, he says, was partly due to his wish to continue the trip with his friends, but he had his own private reasons for not turning back. The next stop was an abandoned geologic settlement—and because Yudin was studying geology at school, he was curious to see what minerals and gemstones he might find amid the deserted buildings.

After a late breakfast, the woodcutters filed out of the cabins to see their new friends off. Boroda emerged with an unruly mane and a cigarette between his fingers. When he realized proper group photographs were being taken, he smoothed back his hair and assumed a pose with his Comrades. As a parting gesture, the hikers presented their hosts with gifts, whatever possessions they thought they could spare. One of the Sector 41 workers, Georgy Ryazhnev, later revealed to investigators, "They presented master Yevgeny Venediktov with a fiction book and gave a present to Anatoly Tutinkov as well."

That afternoon, a Lithuanian named Stanislav Velikyavichus arrived with a horse-drawn sleigh to escort the hikers to the geologic settlement. Velikyavichus was on an errand that day to pick up iron pipes from the abandoned site, and, as luck had it, his sleigh had room enough to hold the hikers' packs. He was a freelance worker at the settlement, and having been imprisoned for six years at Sector 2 of the eighth department of penitentiary camps, he was the travelers' first encounter with a former convict of the region. What Velikyavichus did to earn his imprisonment isn't clear, but, whatever his crime, Sector 41's director didn't see any reason not to put the hikers in his trust. Neither did the hikers, who would affectionately dub him "Grandpa Slava."

Because Velikyavichus arrived so late in the day, the trade-off for a lightened load was that they would be making much of their 15-mile trek by moonlight. The ten skiers said farewell to their woodcutter friends and proceeded north from Sector 41 deeper into the forest. Though they were temporarily relieved of their packs, the skiers had 15 miles of difficult country to cross before reaching the next settlement. To break up the monotony of travel, the friends would stop periodically, and cameras would appear from beneath their coats. A visual record of their progress was crucial in earning their next hiking grade of III. By capturing their journey on film, they could prove to the university that they were complying with the various hiking codes: regulation clothing, proper gear and skiing in proper formation. This didn't stop them from mugging for the camera occasionally, and a fair portion of film was devoted to less serious documentation, including swapping hats and adopting exaggerated poses. A look at their album reveals typical college students clearly enjoying each other's company.

There was thick forest all around them, and the easiest path through the snow was up the frozen Lozva River. Yudin says the ice wasn't very thick, and it wasn't cold enough to completely ensure against their skis penetrating through to the water. What's more, the sticky snow would turn to ice on their skis, compelling them to stop periodically and slice away the ice with a knife. But, in doing so, they had to be careful not to put too much weight on the river. "It was very difficult and dangerous," Yudin remembers. "The river was covered in snow and you couldn't see the ice you were standing on."

Group photo at Sector 41, January 27, 1959.

The Dyatlov hikers en route from Sector 41 to the abandoned geological site. From front to back: Yuri Doroshenko, Zinaida "Zina" Kolmogorova, Lyudmila "Lyuda" Dubinina, Stanislav "Grandpa Slava" Velikyavichus. Yuri Yudin can be seen in the far background, January 27, 1959.

Nikolay "Kolya" Thibault-Brignoles plays in the snow assuming positions of faux distress, January 27, 1959.

From left to right: Lyudmila "Lyuda" Dubinina, Yuri "Georgy" Krivonishchenko, Nikolay "Kolya" Thibault-Brignoles, and Rustem "Rustik" Slobodin, January 27, 1959.

Yuri "Georgy"
Krivonishchenko takes a
photo, January 27, 1959

To keep their energy up, the skiers had purchased four loaves of warm bread at Sector 41, and, over the course of the night, they split two of the loaves among themselves. Meanwhile, Grandpa Slava's horse seemed to move ever more slowly over the perilous river, and despite the skiers' own cautious pace, the Lithuanian and his sleigh eventually disappeared from view behind them.

At last, in the light of the three-quarter moon, the travelers were able to make out a cluster of snow-capped rooftops. As they approached, the settlement seemed to grow into a full village, but there would be no villagers to receive them tonight. There were around twenty cabins, all silent, with no fire or candlelight in a single window. The skiers moved down the trackless streets, past doors and windows that had been left or blown open—and in the moonlight, they could make out the outlines of forsaken stoves and furniture inside. The settlement had been abandoned two or three years before, but, to look at it, one might have imagined the inhabitants of these cabins just having been forced to leave at a moment's notice, having no time to collect their furniture or to latch their doors before leaving their homes forever.

The woodcutters had informed them that only one of the houses was in suitable condition for spending the night, and it took some effort to find it. In his diary, Doroshenko noted the discovery of the house—discernible from the water hole cut in the ice—and the late arrival of Velikyavichus.

> We found it late at night and guessed the location of the hut only by a hole in ice. Made fire out of boards. Stove is smoking. Some of us hurt our hands on the nails. Everything's OK. And the horse arrived. And then, after dinner, in a well-heated hut, we were bantering till 3:00 AM.

The girls took the available beds, and the men—Grandpa Slava included—spread out on the floor with their sleeping bags. Despite the growing pain in his leg, Yudin chose to believe that he'd feel better in the morning.

When Yudin awoke and tried to pull himself off the floor into a standing position, it became apparent to everyone, including Yudin, that it would be foolish for him to continue on the trip. Besides, this was his last opportunity to head safely back to civilization. From here on, there would be no more settlements—only forest—and the group couldn't risk having to carry Yudin out should he be unable to move. And so it was decided that he would return home. Kolya wrote in the group's diary:

> Sure is a pity to part with him, especially to me and Zina, but it can't be helped.

While Grandpa Slava was readying his load of iron pipes to take back to Sector 41, Yudin gathered as many minerals as he could

The abandoned cabin where the Dyatlov hikers stayed,
January 28, 1959.

The Dyatlov hikers rest on the geologists' shelves in the
abandoned village. From left to right: Lyudmila "Lyuda"
Dubinina, Alexander "Sasha" Zolotaryov, Zinaida "Zina"
Kolmogorova, January 28, 1959.

Yuri Yudin shares a final hug with Lyudmila "Lyuda" Dubinina
before returning home. Igor Dyatlov looks on, January 28, 1959.

find scattered around the area, mostly pyrite and quartz, and piled
them into the sleigh. "The man with the horse was in a hurry," Yudin
remembers, "and yelled for me to hurry up." Yudin regretted having
to leave his friends, but he adopted his usual smile and reminded
himself that they'd be reunited in ten days. After a round of warm
hugs, he left the nine to continue the trek to Otorten Mountain
without him. He loaded his pack onto the sleigh, but the extremely
cold pipes prevented him from hitching a ride himself. And so with
aches shooting through his legs and back, Yudin skied after Grandpa
Slava and the horse all the way down the 15 miles of winding river.

★

16

AFTER NEWS OF THE FOUR BODIES REACHES SVERDLOVSK, and the initial shock sets in, friends and family of the hikers begin to cast about for someone to blame. Many hold the university responsible for allowing students to embark on such dangerous expeditions in the first place. There are additional rumblings around this time that investigators should be directing their inquiries toward the native people of the region. When Mansi tracks are discovered not far from the hikers' route, the question arises: Did the tribe resent Russians intruding on their sacred territory? To address the growing suspicions, foresters who work in proximity to the Mansi are brought into Ivdel for questioning.

Forester Ivan Rempel, who had met the hikers in Vizhay a week before their disappearance, is unequivocal in his defense of the Mansi. "I believe it's impossible," he remarks in his testimony of early March, "because I meet Mansi often and don't hear any hostile words toward other nations from them. They are very hospitable when you visit or meet them." Rempel also points out that the area where the hikers traveled is not sacred tribal land. "Local residents say that sacred rocks of the Mansi are at the Vizhay riverhead, 100 to 150 kilometers from the place of the hikers' deaths."

As for signs that the Mansi had been shadowing the hikers, Vizhay forester Ivan Pashin rejects the evidence in his testimony to investigators: "At one kilometer from the first stopping place of the hikers, we saw a Mansi standing site where they pastured reindeer, but it was after the hikers' deaths, because the Mansi tracks were fresh, and the hikers' [camp] looked old." He concludes, "Mansi could not have attacked hikers. On the contrary, knowing their habits, they help Russians. . . . Mansi have taken lost people into their homes and sustained them by providing food."

Andrey Anyamov, a Mansi hunter and reindeer herdsman from Suyevatpaul, had been hunting near the Auspiya River in late January, around the time the hikers had been in the area. When he and his companions are brought to Ivdel for questioning, he tells investigators, "All four of us saw ski tracks, but we didn't follow them. We saw trails of moose, wolves, wolverines, but didn't see fire places or hear human voices." As for the idea that the area held any religious significance for the tribe, Anyamov's hunting partner, Konstantin Sheshkin, points out: "There's no sacred mountain in our hunting places. . . . But now the Mansi don't visit sacred mountains. The youth don't pray at all, and elders pray at home."

After several interviews of this nature, it becomes clear to investigators that, aside from there being zero physical evidence of Mansi involvement, a people known for their harmonious nature could hardly have orchestrated an event that would have sent the hikers to their deaths.

Back on Holatchahl mountain, the search party—which still includes Mansi volunteers—is discarding all hope of finding any of the Dyatlov group alive. This is now a recovery mission, and the searchers are left with the grim task of locating five snowy graves. Maslennikov orders an area of 30,000 square yards to be probed by a team of thirty men. Some of the searchers have been using ski poles to plumb the depths of the snow, but when the probes Maslennikov ordered from his factory arrive, they are able to reach a new depth of over eight feet. The men, clad in near-identical coats and trapper

Search teams probe the area for the hikers, February–March, 1959.

caps arrange themselves in shoulder-to-shoulder chains in front of a patch of ground. Then, steel in hand, they advance over the landscape, stabbing at the snow, like a small army whose enemy is beneath their feet. It is an exhausting and imperfect system, and the men encounter patches where the probes fail to reach the ground. There is one particular ravine that is roughly 15 feet deep. Via radiogram, an official in Ivdel suggests sending miners with metal detectors to the mountains.

Maslennikov replies:

MINERS NEED PROBES RATHER THAN METAL DETECTORS
AS PEOPLE UNDER SNOW DON'T HAVE METAL THINGS.

But Maslennikov's opinion on the matter is ignored, and the next day a team of miners arrives, metal detectors in tow. After a day or two of sweeping the ground and finding nothing, the miners realize that Maslennikov was right. Whatever watches or metal accessories the hikers might have been wearing is not enough to set off the detectors. So the miners trade in their machines for probes and join the files of men stabbing at the snow.

On March 1, Lev Ivanov arrives on the scene. Ivanov is not replacing Tempalov as lead investigator because of any particular incompetence on the latter's part; the discovery of the bodies merely requires a higher level of oversight, and Ivanov's regional scope trumps Tempalov's municipal one. In addition to his title as junior counselor of justice, Ivanov is a World War II veteran, a husband and a father. He is too obsessed with work, however, to be described by his wife and two young daughters as a family man—and that spring, the Dyatlov case will only take him farther away from his family for longer periods of time. In the coming months, as Ivanov makes multiple trips into the northern Urals, the topography around Holatchahl mountain will become forever etched in his mind.

Ivanov's first order of business is to board a helicopter and familiarize himself with the locations where the bodies were discovered. There is little to be seen in the places where Zina and Dyatlov had fallen, but the site of the 25-foot cedar tree yields more clues. Examining the charred cedar branches at the fire pit, Ivanov determines that the fire had not burned for more than two hours. It is also apparent from broken branches found nearby, that one of the men had climbed the tree and had likely fallen in the process of cutting away branches. Cedar trees are dry and fragile, and the bough may have given way beneath him. This would be consistent with the cuts and bruises found on Doroshenko's body, as well as the branches found beneath him. Once the men had started the fire, it would have been large enough to warm them, but not large enough to keep it burning for long. There are also additional footprints, leading Ivanov to believe that at least one other person besides Doroshenko and Krivonishchenko had been present at the site of the tree. There is also evidence of firewood

Lev Ivanov on the
scene, March 1, 1959.

and fir twigs having been gathered for the fire, but not used. The obvious question, then, besides why the hikers had been only half-dressed with no shoes, is: Why gather perfectly good firewood, but let the fire go out? Ivanov records what information he can from the location, and as he heads back up the slope to commence his formal inspection of the tent, he considers the puzzle.

Together with Maslennikov, Ivanov examines the hikers' camp and its immediate surroundings. The two men determine that the tent was erected as per hiking regulations. And though the tent is damaged with multiple tears, its integrity on the slope is intact, having clearly been rooted to the slope to account for strong winds.

Maslennikov, in the meantime, in one of his many daily radiograms to Ivdel, begins to imagine a sequence of events for the night of February 1. He suggests that the hikers had dinner in the tent while still in the day's damp clothes. Then, after nearing the end of dinner, they left the food out as they started changing into their dry clothes and shoes. At the very moment of changing their clothes, something happened to force all nine hikers out into the snow half-dressed.

MAYBE SOMEONE WHO WAS DRESSED WENT OUTSIDE TO TAKE A LEAK AND WAS SWEPT AWAY. HIS CRY MADE OTHERS JUMP OUT OF THE TENT AND THEY WERE SWEPT OFF TOO. TENT IS SET IN MOST DANGEROUS POINT WITH STRONGEST WIND. IMPOSSIBLE TO GO 50 [METERS] BACK UPHILL AS TENT WAS TORN. THOSE WHO WERE BELOW COULD COMMAND TO GO TO FOREST ON SLOPE TOWARD AUSPIYA WHERE FOREST IS NEAR; MAYBE THEY WANTED TO FIND THEIR PREVIOUS CAMP PLACE. SLOPE IS ROCKY AND 2 TO 3 TIMES FARTHER FROM FOREST. THEY MADE A FIRE. AS DYATLOV AND KOLMOGOROVA WERE BETTER DRESSED, THEY WENT BACK TO LOOK FOR THE TENT WITH THEIR CLOTHES. LACKING STRENGTH THEY FELL.

The weather is challenging for the volunteers on the slope that day, with high winds chafing skin and limiting visibility. By evening, the probing has turned up nothing and the searchers are growing increasingly fatigued. Yuri Blinov, who is taking additional time away from school to continue the search, is among those who craved some levity at the end of a day spent looking for corpses. He wrote of this time in his diary:

In the evenings, participants tired from endless probing of snowy slopes returned to the tent and were telling tales in the absence of other business. Officers were entertaining us with all sorts of stories from criminal world routine. Jokes were popular as well.

Though he is dedicated to the search for his missing friends, Blinov is exhausted and worried about skipping so many classes. It is time for him to return to Sverdlovsk. Two days later, Blinov and two other UPI students fly back home to resume their college lives.

The weather on March 2 is little better than the previous day. Probing picks up where it left off, with some of the team expanding its search beyond the river valley. One of Maslennikov's radiograms that day indicates he is rethinking his initial theory as to the hikers' fate:

> WOULD LIKE TO ASK IF ANY NEW TYPE OF METEOROLOGI-
> CAL ROCKET PROBE FLEW OVER INCIDENT PLACE ON
> THE EVENING OF FEBRUARY 1.

It is a cryptic message, and he doesn't explain further, adding only:

> PLEASE SEND BUTTER, HALVA, CONCENTRATED MILK,
> SUGAR, COFFEE, TEA, CIGARETTES.

The following day brings a snowstorm and high winds, but the searchers press on, paying particular attention to the Lozva River valley. Maslennikov also expresses for the first time his belief that the rest of the hikers did not get out alive:

> TEAM REACHED LOZVA. DYATLOV GROUP'S TRACES NOT
> FOUND, SNOW FROM MAIN RIDGE DUMPED INTO THIS
> BROOK, SNOW IS VERY DEEP. PROBABILITY THAT PART
> OF GROUP ESCAPED THROUGH THIS VALLEY TO LOZVA
> IS ZERO. . . .

The severity of the storm forces Maslennikov's group to turn back from the Lozva valley. But another group, which includes Slobtsov and Kurikov, has found the Dyatlov group's storage shelter near the Auspiya River. There is nothing amiss about the structure. It is built to regulation standards and, aside from the meager amount of firewood, is filled with the necessary food and reserves that would have been needed for their return trip. The condition of the shelter only reinforces the searchers' belief that these hikers had stuck religiously to protocol. Among the objects in the shelter is a single sentimental item: Georgy's mandolin. With this abandoned instrument, the groups' dedication to their sport is apparent — in earning their advanced hiking grade, even the music they loved was expendable.

Later that day, Maslennikov and his team gather at the improvised helipad to see Lev Ivanov off. The prosecutor has done what he can at the tent site and will continue the investigation from his office in Sverdlovsk. Accompanying Ivanov in the helicopter are the bodies of Doroshenko, Krivonishchenko, Igor Dyatlov and Zina, all of which will undergo autopsies in the next couple of days.

Ivanov may be the lead investigator, but Maslennikov continues to explore his own theories via radiogram:

> BUT THE MAIN MYSTERY IS WHY THE WHOLE GROUP FLED THE TENT. THE ONLY THING FOUND OUTSIDE THE TENT BESIDE THE ICE PICK IS A CHINESE TORCH ON THE TENT ROOF. THIS PROVES ONE FULLY DRESSED PERSON WENT OUTSIDE AND GAVE SOME SIGNAL TO OTHERS TO FLEE THE TENT AT ONCE.

Maslennikov also clarifies his question about rocket probes:

> ONE POSSIBLE REASON IS SOME NATURAL PHENOMENON OR PASSAGE OF METEOROLOGICAL ROCKET PROBE WHICH WAS SEEN ON FEB. 1 FROM IVDEL AND BY KARELIN'S GROUP ON FEB. 17.

"Karelin's group" refers to the hiking team led by Vladislav Karelin, who is now among the search volunteers. Karelin and his companions had set out in February, shadowing the Dyatlov group's path along the riverbed. At the beginning of the search for the missing hikers, Karelin's visit to a Mansi village in mid-February, in which he and his fellow hikers shared tea with Pyotr Bahtiyarov, had been mistaken for a visit by Igor Dyatlov's group. The mistake, which was eventually corrected, only temporarily misled investigators. But the Karelin group's trip was to become of growing interest in the case. Several days after their visit to the Mansi village, Karelin and his friends had witnessed what he called a "strange celestial phenomenon." Karelin later told investigators that on the early morning of February 17, he had been awoken by excited cries from the hikers on breakfast duty. "I rushed out of my sleeping bag and tent without boots, just in socks, stood on branches and saw a large light spot," he recounted. "It grew larger. A small star appeared in its center and also grew bigger. The whole spot moved from northeast to southwest and down." Karelin said that the light lasted just over a minute, and that he supposed it was a large meteorite. But one of his friends, Georgy Atmanaki, was so terrified by the orb of light, he feared a planet was about to collide with Earth. "I talked with witnesses later," Atmanaki told investigators, "and they described the event similarly and added that the light was so intense that people were awoken inside their houses."

Now Maslennikov wonders: Did Igor Dyatlov and his friends witness something similar? Something that caused them to leave the tent wearing no shoes?

Over the coming days, the evidence grows stranger. On March 5, as Karelin and another volunteer are probing a previously unexplored area, about 1,000 yards from the site of the hikers' tent, they hit something not far beneath the surface: a fifth body. When they dig away the snow, Karelin is able to identify him as Rustik Slobodin. His body is lying facedown with his right leg bent beneath him, and his right fist pulled to his chest. He has on a checkered shirt, sweater, ski trousers, several pairs of socks and a single felt shoe. He also wears a ski cap, which is still intact on his head—strange, given the prevailing theory that wind blew the hikers from their campsite. Rustik lies midway between where Dyatlov and Zina had been found, their bodies in turn lining up with the site of the tent. Like Zina, Rustik is oriented toward the tent as if he had been working his way up the slope at the time of his collapse. Karelin and his companion notice a small hollow of encrusted snow near Rustik's nose and mouth, where his breath had melted the surrounding snow, suggesting that Rustik had been alive for some time after he fell. But what is most startling is the front of Rustik's head, which is deeply discolored, as if he sustained a blunt force to the head.

After pictures are taken and the area thoroughly documented, Rustik's body is moved to the site of Boot Rock to await transport to Sverdlovsk. And now four hikers remain missing: Lyuda Dubinina, Sasha Zolotaryov, Alexander Kolevatov and Kolya Thibault-Brignoles.

Around this time, after the tent's contents are transported to Ivdel for further examination, a discovery is made about the tent itself. The discovery had, in fact, been noted in the case file early on, but it was not initially believed to be significant. Besides the ice-ax gashes made by Mikhail Sharavin upon discovery of the tent, there are additional cuts to the back of the tent. These are not the cuts of an ice ax, but appear to be made with more precision. There is one longer cut that is large enough to accommodate a person stepping through it. When a professional tailor is brought to the prosecutor's office to make a new uniform for one of its officers, the woman is also asked to take a look at the damaged tarpaulin. After examining the threads along the mysterious cut, she confirms what investigators have already concluded: It is a deliberate slash made with a knife. The tailor hesitates to speculate beyond that, but for investigators, the meaning is clear. The hikers themselves would not have damaged their own tent in this way, even by accident, so this seems to suggest one thing: Someone from the outside knifed his way through the tent on that terrible night.

★

17

2012

WHEN WE ARRIVED AT THE TRAIN STATION, IT WAS STILL dark. Kuntsevich's martial discipline had us at the station at eight thirty in the morning, with over an hour to spare. I had been up for three hours, yet was still trying to shake myself out of my medicated daze after having taken a Valium the night before. I was not in the habit of taking pills in order to sleep—the Valium prescription was for my vertigo, a condition I'd been dealing with on and off for the previous seven years. But I had been so wired the previous night that without some help, I wouldn't have slept at all. Even so, I'd slept only a few hours and was now struggling to stay alert on this first day of our trip.

I left my companions for a moment to explore the station. Fifty-three winters ago, the Dyatlov hikers had nearly missed their evening train leaving from Sverdlovsk. I could almost see them hurrying past me toward the platform, breathless, ten pairs of boots squeaking across the marble floors. I thought of Lyuda's younger brother, Igor, walking here months later, after having returned from his studies in Uzbekistan. When I'd interviewed him on my last trip, he told me how he'd left Sverdlovsk in the winter of 1959, but because he hadn't exchanged letters with his family, he had no idea that his sister was missing until he returned that April. He had only to step off the train and see his parents standing there on

157

the platform to know that something was wrong. Though Lyuda's body had not yet been found, her fate was written on their faces.

I wanted to imagine that I was occupying the same space as these people I had come to know, but the truth was that this building had been rebuilt and renovated over the years, and must have looked very different in 1959. There was an even older station to the west, a candy-colored artifact of imperial Russia that predated the hikers, which was now a railway museum. This particular station was most recently refurbished in 2003, with many of the old murals having been restored and a few new ones added.

In the vaulted waiting room, I studied the murals on the walls and ceilings, which made plain just how much had changed over the decades. There was a mural of the Romanov family's celestial ascent, the Red and White armies positioned on either side. I would learn later that this image—featuring the seven Romanovs being pulled skyward, as if by tractor beam—reflected the family's canonization by the Russian Orthodox Church in the year 2000. What would Yudin, who was still sentimental about Communist Russia, make of it? Even stranger was a mural reminiscent of a Depression-era WPA project. Similar in composition to the Romanov image, it featured two sets of Soviets—scientists on the left and military men on the right. Front and center were the smoking pieces of a plane falling from a blue sky, an American flag visible on a torn wing. Tumbling beside the wing was the plane's ejected pilot, Gary Powers. Not depicted in the mural was how, instead of injecting himself with the saxitoxin-tipped needle he carried, Powers was instead captured, interrogated for months by the KGB and ultimately convicted of espionage and sentenced to ten years in prison. But less than a year later, the pilot was exchanged in a spy swap for Soviet agent Rudolf Abel. The US government had originally denied the existence of Powers's aircraft—blaming the incident on a weather plane that had drifted off course into Soviet airspace—only to sheepishly admit to lying about the whole affair after Khrushchev declared: "I must tell you a secret. When I made my first report, I deliberately did not say that the pilot was alive and well . . . and now just look how many silly things the Americans have said."

As I stood there, below the image of a U-2 spy plane falling to earth, I calculated that Powers would have been grounded exactly fifteen months after the Dyatlov hikers perished. My brain, I realized, needed to connect everything back to the hikers, no matter how tangential.

The station was becoming busy, though I didn't notice anyone besides us hauling around backpacks and ski equipment. The life of a *tourist* evidently wasn't what it had been during Khrushchev's Thaw, and no one here seemed to think it a good idea to go marching in the general direction of Siberia in the middle of winter. As our departure time drew near, I purchased a handful of Russian chocolate bars from a station vendor, stowing them in my pack as a reward for when we reached the location of the tent. When I rejoined my companions, I took out my point-and-shoot, intent on getting a departing shot of the station. But as I was about to snap a shot of the lobby, Kuntsevich and Borzenkov reached out their hands to block the lens. Photos were not welcome in the station, though without a translator, they had difficultly telling me why.

Before we boarded the train, we met the fourth member of our group, Dmitri Voroshchuk, a recruit of Kuntsevich's. Beneath his manicured beard and wire-rimmed glasses, I could see that he was in his late-thirties, tops, no older than me. In his modest English, Voroshchuk explained that he was a professional geologist who had a strong interest in the case and a love of the Ural Mountains.

I was pleased with our four-man group, as we each had a specific purpose. As an outdoor disaster expert with an emphasis on avalanche studies, and having served as vice president of the Union Federation of Tourism, Borzenkov would be our navigator.

Voroshchuk, although not a professional interpreter, knew enough English to allow us to communicate more clearly. And because he was also a geologist, he would be able to give us insights into the topography of the area. Kuntsevich, with his twenty-five years of intimate knowledge of the case, and scout leadership skills, was clearly the team leader. And finally, being the observer of the group, I was the natural pick for team diarist. I was also the first American, so I was told, to attempt this particular trek to the northern Ural Mountains in the winter.

There were beds on both sides of the train car: bunk beds on one side, single Murphy beds on the other. We stowed our packs in the overhead racks and made our way to the apple-red benches lining the cars. Before I could take my seat, Kuntsevich cordially placed the standard white sheets and blue pillowcases, handed to us upon boarding, beneath us. We pulled out the foldout tables and poured ourselves tea from a thermos. We settled in and tried to pretend that we weren't all completely on top of one another, and when we brought our plastic cups to our lips, we took special care not to knock our elbows into our neighbor's tea.

Although we were traveling in a third-class common carriage, or *platzkart*, our comfort level was much higher than that of the Dyatlov hikers. As Borzenkov explained to me, their carriages would have been wooden and without upholstery. Heating was available to them, but not like the steam bath we were currently experiencing in our bulky winter outfits. In addition to their having traveled on a much slower train, the Dyatlov group had to switch trains in Serov; whereas we'd be traveling directly to Ivdel with a stopover in Serov.

As the train left Yekaterinburg, the sun was just beginning to rise, casting its glow over the cheek-by-jowl city of old and new, of pastel masonry and glass. Borzenkov wasted no time in pulling out his artist's pad to illustrate the route we'd be taking, and how it compared with the Dyatlov route. I'd brought a small notebook and a pencil broken in half to save space. I had jettisoned my pen after Borzenkov informed me that ballpoints were unreliable in subzero temperatures; the ink would freeze.

For lunch, Kuntsevich produced a container of what resembled a purple Jell-O dessert, but instead of fruit, it was stuffed with herring, potatoes, boiled beets and mayonnaise—all topped with slices of onion. The name of the dish, "herring under a fur coat," was a pretty accurate way of describing how it felt on one's tongue, and when I was offered some, I took the politest of bites. To my relief, I had a meal of my own. Olga had slipped me a bag before we left, which contained my favorite chicken dish. I downed it hungrily between gulps of tea.

After our meal, a satiated silence settled over our group. I stared out of my window and watched old power lines fly by, their poles sticking out of the snow at odd angles, like giant crosses. I rarely travel by train in my own country, but when I have, I've noticed the hypnotic effect it produces. The thundering below put me in a meditative state as I reflected on the past couple of weeks in Yekaterinburg. They'd been mostly encouraging, and I had been extraordinarily lucky to get to know the famously reclusive Yuri Yudin.

But my trip had not been entirely positive. Earlier in the week, a reporter from a Yekaterinburg TV station had shown up at Kuntsevich's apartment to interview me. Through a translator, he had repeatedly asked me how much money I was making from my book—the implication evidently being that I had come all this way to exploit a foreign mystery for profit. Money was not a factor in my visit to his country, I told him, resisting the temptation to laugh at the idea that one gets rich in publishing. I also resisted telling him that I'd had no notion of a book deal when I'd begun the project. And I didn't tell him how conflicted

I felt about having self-financed this entire three-year endeavor, maxing out credit cards and draining my savings account—all the while starting a family.

The reporter had continued with his questions: "What if you don't feel anything if and when you make it to the location where the hikers died?" and "Why would you, an American, care about Russian hikers who died long before you were born?" I had answered these questions as best I could, without getting too defensive. Still, the reporter's interrogation lingered long after the interview ended, as if he had gotten at something I was afraid of examining.

Over the past weeks of interviewing Yudin and reviewing my case notes, I was coming to the conclusion that the reason for the hikers fleeing the tent had nothing at all to do with weapons, men with guns or related conspiracies. Avalanche statistics were incredibly convincing: Nearly 80 percent of ski-related deaths were the result of avalanches. Wasn't it the likeliest theory, after all? I imagined how the hikers would have heard the terrifying rumble of unsettled snow above their campsite, and would have fled from their tent in panic. But once they were outside in subzero air with a fierce wind pushing them down the slope, the elements had done the rest. Were all my efforts really leading to the simplest explanation of all? Until we were on the slope itself, there was little for me to do but focus on the journey ahead and on our next stop: Serov.

Kuntsevich told me that we were the first hikers to be following the Dyatlov party's itinerary, and the first to visit the school in Serov for that purpose. But because we had no address for the school—we knew only that in 1959 it bore the name School #41— it would not be easy to find. To make things trickier, Igor and his friends had stayed in Serov the entire day, whereas our stop would be only ninety minutes.

I felt a nap coming on and claimed one of the bunk beds. My companions did the same. Before I fell asleep, I turned to the window and was reminded of the diary entry Zina had written on their first night on the train—something about the Ural Mountains looming in the distance. And then there was her final question of the night: "I wonder what awaits us on this hike? Will anything new happen?" The thick air of the car finally put me to sleep. But the slow heartbeat of the train kept my slumber fitful as we drew ever closer to the place where Zina's diary entries had come to an end.

Zinaida "Zina" Kolmogorova writes in her diary, Auspiya River,
January 29, 1959.

★

18

AFTER THEY WATCHED THEIR AILING FRIEND RECEDE WITH Grandpa Slava and his horse down the Lozva, the remaining nine hikers turned in the opposite direction and continued their trek upriver. Their path over the next few days would cleave to the rivers—first the Lozva, and then the adjoining Auspiya, which they would follow north toward Otorten Mountain. Their second day on the Lozva was not all that different from the first, and they progressed over the snow-covered ice in determined silence. But because Yuri Yudin was now gone, only the film in their cameras and the pages of their diaries could bear witness to these final days of their journey.

When the path through the snow became particularly punishing, the friends would alternate taking the lead, with each shift as leader lasting ten minutes. Besides that, they had to pause every so often to scrape congealed snow from the bottoms of their skis. Where the ice on the river became dangerously thin, or where the water leached through, the skiers were forced onto the riverbank. But when the bank was too steep, or covered in jagged patches of basalt, they were forced to choose the lesser danger: fragile ice or treacherous terrain.

Their progress became considerably easier when they happened upon an existing path made by skis and reindeer hooves, the telltale sign of Mansi hunters. There were also Mansi symbols painted on the trees along their route, as described in the group's diary:

> [*The symbols*] *are kinds of forest stories. The marks describe animals noticed, stand sites, various indicators, and decoding those marks would be of great interest both to hikers and to historians.*

In the evenings, each member of the group had his or her assigned task in setting up camp before they were allowed to gather by the stove for dinner. As on previous nights, there was music and passionate discussion. Kolya described the group's first night in the tent:

> *After dinner, we sit a long time by the fire, singing sincere songs. Zina even tries to learn playing mandolin under the guidance of our chief musician Rustemka. Then discussion goes on and on, and almost all our discussions these days deal with love.*

When the friends became sleepy, they couldn't come to an agreement about who should lie next to the stove. An outsider might have assumed that a spot nearest the source of warmth would be the most coveted. But according to Kolya's diary, the portable stove that divided the tent was "blazing." While he and Zina occupied the area farthest from it, Georgy and Kolevatov were persuaded to sleep on either side of it.

> [*Georgy*] *lay for about two minutes, then he could not stand it anymore and retreated to the far end of the tent cursing terribly and blaming us for treachery. After that, we stayed awake for a long time, arguing about something, but finally it went still.*

The next day was less eventful, and after hours of making their way up the second river, their group diary had little to say:

Carved tree with painted Mansi symbols. The first three slashes represent the number of hunters in the group. The second symbol represents the family sign and the third set of slashes represents the number of dogs in the Mansi group, January 29, 1959.

The Dyatlov hikers stop for a rest. Left to right: Alexander "Sasha" Zolotaryov, Yuri Doroshenko and Igor Dyatlov, eating "salo," January 30, 1959.

Second day of skiing. From our night camp by the Lozva River we took the route to the night camp at Auspiya River, along a Mansi path. Weather is fine, −13°. Weak wind. There is often an ice crust on the Lozva. That's all.

On the third day, their trek became markedly more difficult. The temperature dropped, a southwest wind began to blow, and snow fell. What's more, the group lost the Mansi tracks. With the benefit of an already trodden path now gone, and with the snowpack almost four feet deep in places, their progress slowed considerably. Meanwhile the forest seemed to be retreating around them. The trees thinned, and the remaining birches and pines shrank to a dwarfish size and began to appear out of the ground at crooked, windblown angles. Despite the drop in temperature, the ice on the river was still too thin to rely on:

It's impossible to go over the river, it's not frozen. Water and ice crust are under the snow right on the ski track, so we go near the shore again.

Though they had lost the Mansi's path, the hikers continued to find symbols among the dwindling trees. As the group's diary records, they talked increasingly of the native people.

Mansi, Mansi, Mansi. This word becomes more frequent in our talks. Mansi are people of the North. . . . It's a very interesting and peculiar nation living in northern Urals, close to Tyumen region.

Zina was particularly fascinated by the tribal symbols and stopped to copy some of them in her diary.

The Dyatlov hikers travel up the Lozva River. Front to
back: Nikolay "Kolya" Thibault-Brignoles, Alexander "Sasha"
Zolotaryov, and Lyudmila "Lyuda" Dubinina (left), January 30, 1959.

*Maybe the title of our trip should be "In the land of mysterious
signs." If we knew their meaning, we could follow the path without
worrying that it might take us in the wrong direction.*

After a late afternoon meal of leftovers from breakfast—brisket,
dried bread, sugar, garlic, coffee—they continued on for another
few hours before stopping for the night. But with the landscape
increasingly exposed, the group had to double back over 200 yards
to find a suitable spot surrounded by tall, dry trees. It had been a
difficult day, perhaps the most difficult yet, and for some among
the group, tempers were short. An argument erupted between
Lyuda and Kolya concerning one of their chores. Zina bore witness to the episode:

So they argued for a long time about who should stitch the tent. At last [Kolya] gave up and took a needle. Lyuda remained sitting. And we were fixing holes (so many holes that everyone had plenty to do. . . . The guys are awfully indignant.

Later that night, the mood brightened as the group gathered around an outdoor fire to celebrate Doroshenko's twenty-first birthday. They presented him with a gift that had been stowed away for the occasion: a tangerine. Tangerines had been available in the Soviet Union since the 1930s when they began to be shipped north from the Abkhazia citrus plantations near the Black Sea. They were a special fruit available only for a brief season, and because of their aura of novelty, they were often given as gifts around New Year's Day. But instead of enjoying his present, Doroshenko insisted on dividing the tangerine equally among his friends. Only Lyuda missed out on the treat, as she was still stinging from the earlier argument and had sequestered herself in the tent. Zina wrote: "Lyuda had gone inside the tent and didn't appear till the end of dinner." But Zina ended her diary entry on an optimistic, if cautious, note: "So, one more day passed by safely."

The next day, January 31, would be the final day documented in the group's journals. The hikers often wrote their diary entries in the mornings, which meant that they were writing about events of the previous day. Of the last day in January, Igor noted that the group set out at 10:00 AM, and that the weather had immediately worsened with an aggressive wind blowing in from the west. The sky was clear, yet it was inexplicably snowing—but, as Igor noted, the precipitation was most likely an illusion caused by the wind sweeping snow from the treetops.

It was on this second-to-last day of their trip that the nine hikers began to deviate from the river and make their way up the slope in the direction of Otorten Mountain. The group had been lucky in rediscovering the Mansi tracks—ski tracks this time—but the uphill path was still slow going and the hikers needed a more efficient method of cutting through the snow. They invented one on the spot, one that Igor called "path-treading," in which the lead hiker takes off his backpack and beats a path for five minutes before returning to his pack to rest. When he has retrieved his pack, he catches up with the others who have since flattened the path. At the end of the path, they repeat the process with a new leader. Still, even with this method, Igor noted that it was difficult to advance.

> *The track is hardly visible, we lose it often or walk blindly, so we cover only 1.5 to 2 km in an hour.*

Of the wind blowing in their faces, he wrote:

> *The wind is warm and piercing, blows fast like air when a plane takes off.*

The hikers were understandably exhausted, and at 4:00 PM they began to look for a place to set up camp. They went south to the Auspiya valley where the wind was weak and the snow less deep. The downside to the valley was that firewood was scarce, with mostly damp firs at hand. With what firewood they could gather, they chose not to dig a fire pit and simply laid the fire on top of some logs. They ate dinner inside the tent, inspiring Igor to write, in what would be the group's final diary entry:

> *It's hard to imagine such a cozy place anywhere at the ridge, under the piercing howls of the wind, and hundreds of km from any settlements.*

★

FEBRUARY 1

THE FRIENDS TOOK APPROXIMATELY TEN PHOTOGRAPHS on their final day of life, and judging from the first few snapshots taken at the campsite that morning, spirits were high. A casual shot of Kolya and Doroshenko reveals them laughing in front of the tent, surrounded by piles of backpacks. Then there are two images of Rustik, wearing a jacket that looks to have been shredded violently. Upon closer inspection, however, it appears that the material was burned, perhaps when left too close to the stove. If Rustik was worried about losing a much-needed layer of warmth, he doesn't show it in these photographs, and instead adopts a pose of inflated pride. After all, of the nine hikers, Rustik would have been most able to afford a replacement jacket when he got home.

The morning's mood was evidently contagious, and one member of the group drafted the front page of a mock newspaper called *The Evening Otorten*, dated February 1, Issue 1. Among its contents was an editorial posing the question, "Is it possible to keep nine hikers warm with one stove and one blanket?" plus an announcement for a daily seminar titled "Love and Hiking" to be held in the tent by lecturers "Dr." Kolya and "Candidate of Science" Lyuda. The sports page announced that "Comrades Doroshenko and Zina Kolmogorova set a new world record in competition for stove assembly," while the science pages claimed that the "snow man," or yeti, dwelled in the northern Urals around Otorten Mountain.

With the morning's entertainment out of the way, a serious task lay ahead: constructing a *labaz*, or temporary storage shelter. The hikers' packs needed to be as light as possible for their journey up the mountain, and items that weren't crucial for the next two days

Rustem "Rustik" Slobodin shows off his burned jacket.
Perhaps he left it to dry too close to the fire the
previous night, January 31, 1959.

Alexander Kolevatov (left) and Nikolay "Kolya" Thibault-Brignoles share a laugh at the campsite on the morning of January 31, 1959.

At left: Igor Dyatlov, Nikolay "Kolya" Thibault-Brignoles, and Alexander "Sasha" Zolotaryov as they prepare to leave the labaz shelter site under worsening weather, February 1, 1959.

had to be stowed for their return trip. After the shelter's construction, the hikers stocked it with food reserves, extra skis and boots, a spare first aid kit, and—most painfully—Georgy's mandolin. Between selecting items for the shelter and stowing firewood for the night of their return, a significant portion of the morning was gone; and, after the shelter was secure, they were eager to push ahead.

The remaining photographs taken that day reveal the nine friends struggling through a terrain of increasingly sparse trees and blinding weather. There are no jocular photos left, just a group of serious young people determined to conquer a challenging landscape. Two of the images reveal the group skiing single file into a gray haze.

Sunset would come at 4:58 that day, with twilight at 5:52, but because of the heavy cloud cover, they thought it best to set up camp early to avoid getting caught in the dark. They chose a spot on an east-facing slope, which would allow them to pack up quickly in the

The skiers advance to the location of their final campsite. This is one of the last shots taken by the Dyatlov group, February 1, 1959.

morning and head straight up the mountain. It took several hours to set up camp, and the hikers were in the tent by 9:00 PM, ready for the next day's climb. But the nine would never see the summit of Otorten. In fact, they would never set foot on the mountain at all. The worst night of their lives lay in front of them, and not one of them would live to see the sun rise.

★

19

INVESTIGATORS IN IVDEL WEREN'T ABOUT TO SUBMIT the word of a dressmaker into evidence, but her belief that the cuts to the tent had been intentional prompted another woman, scientific officer and criminal expert G. Churkina, to take a closer look. Disregarding the ice-ax gashes that had been made to the roof of the tent upon its discovery—and the various holes patched by the hikers themselves—Churkina focused on three tears at the back panel opposite the entrance. She was able to quickly confirm that the tears were, in fact, cuts. "Usually a tear spreads along the line of less resistance, i.e., either warp or weft threads are torn," she wrote in her report. "Such defects are usually very even, with straight angles. A cut always damages both thread types at various angles. It is impossible to cut only warp threads or only weft threads."

Lev Ivanov and his investigators believed that the case rested on identifying the cause of these gashes, and when the tent had been initially brought in for examination, the condition of the fabric had suggested to some that there had been an outside attacker that night. The determination that the tears had been made by a knife seemed to support this theory, but upon closer examination of the threads under a microscope, Churkina made another discovery: The cuts had come from *inside* the tent. "The defects continue as thin scratches in the corners of the punctures on the internal side

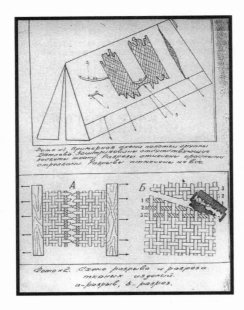

Diagrams from the criminal case files. Top image: "The approximate scheme of the Dyatlov group's tent. Missing fabric pieces are cross-hatched. Cuts are marked by red arrows. Not all tears are marked." Bottom image: "Scheme of fabric tear and cut. A) tear, b) cut."

The Dyatlov hikers' tent in the prosecutor's office for examination, 1959.

of the tent," she wrote, "not on the external side. Nature and form of damage indicate that the cuts were made from inside by some blade/knife."

Once the incisions were determined to have come from the opposite direction, new theories began to emerge. Yuri Blinov, who wrote of the development in his diary, was among those who speculated that the hikers had been caught by surprise by something or someone, and therefore had had no time to completely undo the latches at the entrance. "The tent was cut by a knife from inside in 3 places," Blinov wrote. "It means that *they* were escaping the tent in panic."

The forensic examinations of Igor, Zina, Georgy and Doroshenko on March 4, and of Rustik on March 11, would conclude that the five hikers had died from hypothermia. This was an unsurprising conclusion, particularly to those who had found the bodies. The question now was not how they died, but under what circumstances. But if investigators were hoping that the remaining corpses would provide additional clues, they were in for a long wait. Miserable weather, weary volunteers and the March 8 Soviet holiday celebrating International Working Women's Day slowed search efforts on the slope. In early March, Maslennikov flew to Ivdel to make an appearance in front of the search commission. With the unanimous support of his men, the engineer recommended that search efforts be suspended until April to allow some of the snowpack to melt. The commission, however, rejected Maslennikov's proposal, opting instead to replace the entire search team and continue as planned.

The commission chose Ural Polytechnic Institute physics professor Abram Kikoin, brother of famed Soviet nuclear physicist Isaak Kikoin, to lead the new team. Kikoin was an avid mountaineer and head of the university's mountaineering club, which meant he had immediate access to the best volunteers. But once on the slope, Kikoin and his team encountered the same problems that Maslennikov had. The men battled daily against squall winds, deep snow and myopic visibility, turning up no immediate sign of the remaining four hikers.

During the first week of March, while search efforts were stalling in the mountains, Yuri Yudin took time away from his studies to travel to Ivdel. Because he was one of the few people who knew all nine hikers, he had been summoned by investigators to identify their belongings. It was Ivanov who met Yudin at the Ivdel prosecutor's office, and it was the investigator's kindness that helped him get through the distressing process. "He was a good, caring person," Yudin says of the lead investigator. "He told me, 'Your conscience is clear—if you were with them, you would have been number ten.'"

The searchers on the slope had gathered up the contents of the hikers' tent haphazardly, having stuffed items into backpacks with little regard to ownership. "Everything was in a giant pile," Yudin remembers of entering the office. The task of untangling the mass of objects and assigning each one to its proper owner fell entirely on him. It was a solemn procedure, and the head of the UPI physical training department and a reporter from *Na Smenu!* newspaper were both present as witnesses.

One by one, Yudin separated the items into nine piles.

```
TELESCOPIC TOOTHBRUSH . . . ZINA.
HORN-RIMMED GLASSES IN GRAY CASE . . . IGOR.
BOWIE KNIFE AND COMPASS . . . KOLYA.
MANDOLIN WITH SPARE STRING . . . GEORGY.
GRAY WOOLEN SOCKS RECEIVED AS A PRESENT FROM
    YUDIN . . . LYUDA.
CHECKED VICUÑA SCARF . . . DOROSHENKO.
HIKING BADGE . . . LYUDA.
```

ISSUE OF THE SATIRICAL MAGAZINE KROKODIL . . .
SASHA.
BLUE MITTENS . . . ZINA.
TEDDY BEAR . . . GEORGY.

Yudin encountered all of the familiar items, but there were surprises too. In Kolevatov's backpack, along with a broken comb, a grindstone and an aluminum flask, Yudin found a bit of contraband: a pack of flavored cigarettes. It looked as if the cunning Kolevatov had managed to feed his nicotine addiction after all, the no-smoking pledge be damned. And in Igor's notebook, Yudin discovered a photograph of Zina tucked inside. Had Igor simply been using the snapshot of his friend as a bookmark? Or did this mean something more? It was now, of course, impossible to know. And so it went, until some time later, there lay a diminished pile of clothing and miscellaneous tools to which Yudin was unable to assign an owner.

He left the Ivdel office emotionally spent, but the journey's heartache was not yet over. On the ride back to Sverdlovsk, he shared a helicopter with a woman who was transporting some of the hikers' organs to Sverdlovsk. Yudin remembers the ride as deeply unsettling, as he was painfully aware of the grim contents of the nearby containers.

While the organs were being returned to Sverdlovsk for further analysis, the hikers' families were encountering resistance in getting the bodies of their loved ones returned to them for a proper burial. Now, in addition to wrestling with their own feelings of grief and guilt, the parents of the dead had to contend with the opaque motives of local officials.

Yudin remembers that the regional authorities were eager to get beyond the entire incident, and in private talks with family members, strongly suggested that their loved ones be buried in the mountains. The officials wanted "for nobody to come to the funeral, for nobody to show up," Yudin says. "The authorities wanted to bury them where they were found so there would be no funeral and it would be done."

Rimma Kolevatova, the older sister of Kolevatov, in her testimony to investigators, called the organization of the funeral arrangements "disgraceful." The search teams had not yet found her brother, but she was keenly aware of the ordeal the other families had endured. The parents of the hikers, she recalled, had been summoned by Party officials into private meetings, in which they were told their children should not be returned to Sverdlovsk, but buried instead in Ivdel. "They lived and studied and made friends in Sverdlovsk," Rimma told investigators. "Why should they be buried in Ivdel?" According to Rimma, in these private meetings, each set of parents had been told that the other parents had already agreed to an Ivdel burial, with a mass grave and single obelisk marker. When the parents of Zina Kolmogorova proposed that all the families should be called together to come to an agreement, the secretary of the institute committee of the regional Communist party made excuses that the families were too spread out to make a single meeting feasible.

"What kind of conspiracy is that?" Kolevatov's sister asked. "Why should we go through so many hardships . . . in order to have our relatives buried in their native Sverdlovsk? This is a heartless attitude to people suffering such grave loss. Such an offense to mothers and fathers who had lost their children, good and decent people."

Yudin similarly recalls the families being infuriated with regional officials. "The families wrote letters and were in an uproar to have their funeral in the city." He remembers them insisting: "We want to visit our families, our kids. We want to visit them at their graves."

When the families stood their ground, demanding the return of the bodies, a compromise was reached between city authorities and the parents of the deceased. They would be allowed to bury their children in Sverdlovsk, but under the condition that the funeral not be a single event. The memorial services, they stipulated, would be divided into two services held on two separate days. Minimizing the funeral turnout, and therefore minimizing the deaths of the young hikers, was the authorities' express intention, Yudin says. "They wanted to pretend that nothing happened."

★

20

2012

MY COMPANIONS AND I HAD LESS THAN TWO HOURS TO find School #41 and be back in our seats before the train departed. The trains here, I was told, were Mussolini punctual. Much of Russia's industry had been privatized, but the railway system remained stubbornly state owned. We dared not put its efficiency to the test.

As we stepped out into Serov, I looked back at the old pre-Revolution station, pleased to see that the masonry structure hadn't been rebuilt since the Dyatlov group set foot here. On that January morning in 1959, the attendants hadn't allowed any of the passengers inside the station, and the ten weary hikers had been forced to look for shelter elsewhere. School #41 had become their impromptu hotel. We had no idea if the school still existed, but Kuntsevich suggested that we set out on foot toward the most concentrated area of town. We headed down a snowy road bordered by rustic houses and winter-beaten trees with their tops sawed off. I noticed that the log-cabin-style houses we were passing were the very same ones that appeared in the photographs Igor and his friends took here—images I had developed from the negatives Kuntsevich had given me on my previous trip. I remembered a slightly blurred picture of the oldest member of their group, Sasha Zolotaryov, standing between two such log houses, a duffel bag slung over his shoulder. Next, there was an image of a mother and her adolescent daughter, posing obediently for the camera, their heads wrapped in snug winter scarves.

Along the way we came upon convenience shops that sold common items such as combs, lotions and toothbrushes. We stopped at one or two of these shops to ask for directions, but when Kuntsevich inquired about the school, the proprietors only shook their heads. I remembered from the hikers' diary entries that the station had been fairly close to the school, close enough for the children to have followed the hikers back to their train. If we didn't come across something soon, we'd have to try the other end of town. But about a quarter mile down the road, we found a building that stood out amid the houses. It was three stories of concrete painted a faded yellow, with red-framed windows and a peeling blue fence. There was nothing to indicate that this was a school, but the primary colors of the place seemed to evoke childhood. When I took a closer look at the windows, I could make out the universal sign of an elementary school: paper snowflakes taped to glass.

We entered the building and found a security guard at the front desk. Voroshchuk and Kuntsevich made their inquiries, and after a moment, Kuntsevich gave me the signal that this was indeed School #41. Through Voroshchuk, I learned that the security guard was surprised by our visit: No one had ever come to ask about the hikers, at least not since he'd started working there. After a moment's hesitation, he agreed to accompany us on a quick tour of the building.

As we started down the main corridor, the first thing I noticed was that the building was oddly empty for a Tuesday afternoon. There were no children in sight and, aside from the guard, no staff that I could see. Like many of the Russian buildings I'd been in, the place felt suspended in time. The walls were painted in a two-tone parfait of lime green and off-white, a color scheme not unlike that of the hikers' dorms. I later learned that this particular shade of green was often used in Soviet public spaces because of its durability and low cost.

The time-capsule nature of the building, and the absence of children and teachers, allowed me to easily project Igor and his friends into this space. I stepped away from my companions for a moment to stick my head into an empty classroom. I had no way of knowing which room the hikers had visited, but this one would do as well as any other. I imagined the ten hikers assembled at the head of the room, thirty pairs of eyes watching them with rapt attention. Sasha and Zina had been the stars that day—Sasha with his brief lecture about hiking, and later his playful song. Zina, of course, had won the children over with her general ease and magnetic personality. Yudin's diary entry had even captured humorous scraps of their dialogue:

> Sasha: "Children, we'll tell you about . . . Hiking is . . . provides opportunities . . ." (Kids are sitting silent in fear.)

> Zina: "Blah-blah-blah, you there, what's your name, where did you go? Oh great, you even stayed in tents!" (and so on, and so forth).

I was eager to ask the guard if he knew anything more about the group passing through here, but just as this thought occurred to me, a man came in from outside, and told us we had to leave—immediately. He then asked us for our "papers." I didn't stick around to find out who the man was, as I had unwisely left my passport and Russian invitation on the train. I managed to slip away from the others and out a side door before he noticed me.

After reboarding the train, Kuntsevich told me we were very lucky to have found the school. The Dyatlov group, he said, were "with us in spirit."

★

WE PULLED INTO IVDEL JUST BEFORE MIDNIGHT. AS I peered out the windows of the train, a sense of unease came over me: The buildings were dark and the clouds veiled any existing moonlight. My creeping sense of foreboding had likely little to do with the darkness and more to do with the town's history, of which I had been able to learn a little before my trip. We were now in Gulag territory. In Stalin's time, and for decades afterward, there had been nearly a hundred labor camps in Ivdel—most of them devoted to the incarceration and torture of political dissidents.

In his 1973 "literary investigation," *The Gulag Archipelago*, Solzhenitsyn exposed the practices of the Soviet penal system: "If the intellectuals in the plays of Chekhov who spent all their time guessing what would happen in twenty, thirty or forty years had been told that in forty years interrogation by torture would be practiced in Russia; that prisoners would have their skulls squeezed within iron rings, that a human being would be lowered into an acid bath; that they would be trussed up naked to be bitten by ants and bedbugs; that a ramrod heated over a primus stove would be thrust up their anal canal (the 'secret brand'); that a man's genitals would be slowly crushed beneath the toe of a jackboot; and that, in the luckiest possible circumstances, prisoners would be tortured by being kept from sleeping for a week, by thirst, and by being beaten to a bloody pulp, not one of Chekhov's plays would have gotten to its end because all the heroes would have gone off to insane asylums."

The Gulags of Solzhenitsyn's description were gone, but Ivdel's economy still revolved around the penal system. Because of the moratorium placed on the death penalty in 1996, convicts who would have otherwise been executed were now serving out life sentences in the country's most remote prison camps. One maximum-security prison just outside of Ivdel is still home to some of Russia's worst criminals—though today, their offenses are mostly of a violent nature instead of a political one.

When I stepped onto the station platform, the darkness was startling, with the only light coming from the train and a few station lights. My companions and I walked down the street to await the arrival of what I was told would be our "military transport" to the village of Ushma. Kuntsevich warned that the road there would be quite rough, and that even if the weather cooperated, we wouldn't get there until early morning. We would be taking a slightly different route than the hikers did fifty-three years ago, only passing near what had been the woodcutting settlement of Sector 41. The settlement had long since been demolished and there would be nothing to see, even if we were to stop there. As we waited for our transport, I realized that though we weren't tracing the hikers' steps precisely, this ride would be similar to the one Yudin had endured with his growing back and leg pain.

Thirty minutes later, the headlights of our transport appeared, and a white van with a leather bra cover rolled up in front of the station. Other than a set of impressive tires and a high-beam spotlight on the roof that looked ready to blind every creature within a 50-yard radius, the vehicle looked more like a souped-up '70s Volkswagen than anything out of the Russian military. The inside was outfitted with a metal bench and bucket seats bolted to a floral carpeted floor. Kuntsevich claimed shotgun to better help the driver, while the rest of us climbed in the back. With our gear piled on the carpet, Kuntsevich shut the side door and we were off.

We once again found ourselves in darkness. The windows were blacked out from the inside with a kind of camouflage covering. It was unlikely we'd be passing any lighted streets, but I held out hope that a bit of light, moonlight even, would filter in to give me something to focus on. But as the vehicle pulled away, I quickly realized that my claustrophobia was here for the duration. As I tried to transfer my attention from myself to the goal ahead, memories of previous vertigo spells began to assert themselves. Just a few months before, one of my spells had landed me in the hospital for overnight observation. Vertigo can manifest itself as nausea, vomiting and loss of equilibrium. I tend to experience all three. With my last attack, I had been useless for forty-eight hours, either curled up in bed or positioned over a toilet bowl, completely unable to focus and barely able to walk. I had been so dehydrated from repeated vomiting that during my ambulance ride to the hospital, paramedics had been unable to locate a vein in which to pump fluids into my system.

I hadn't told Kuntsevich or Borzenkov of my preexisting condition. Either I hadn't seen the need to or I didn't want to give them a reason to dismiss me. I had planned to stay alert on this journey, but this dark rumbling box was starting to feel like a moving coffin. So without a word to my companions, I popped a pill and lay back on the bench. As I waited for a Valium-induced sleep to arrive, I wondered if the young Yuri Yudin would have continued with his friends to Otorten Mountain had he been in possession of such powerful drugs. Lucky for him, he only had aspirin.

Funeral procession to Mikhaylovskoye Cemetery, March 9, 1959.

★

21

IN THE SECOND WEEK OF MARCH, TEN DAYS AFTER THE first bodies were discovered in the snow, five of the hikers were buried in Sverdlovsk. The parents had won the right to bury their children in their hometown, but in a final sleight of hand, local party officials controlled how the funerals would be observed. The services were ordered to be split over two days, and when the mourners asked that the procession for the first funeral be allowed to proceed past the UPI campus, located just south of the cemetery, the police refused permission and instead had the caskets directed from the morgue to the Mikhaylovskoye Cemetery via the shortest, least conspicuous route. The message from the police and city officials was clear: Large crowds of mourners and any resulting publicity were unwelcome.

As Yuri Yudin was still in Ivdel helping investigators identify his friends' belongings, he did not attend the funerals. But twelve-year-old Yuri Kuntsevich, the future founder and president of the Dyatlov Foundation, had a front-row seat for the entire event. He lived with his parents and two older brothers in an apartment directly across from the Mikhaylovskoye Cemetery, and had only to look out the window to see the open caskets on flatbed trucks and the sea of mourners trailing behind. There was no fence enclosing the cemetery, and the crowd descending on Mikhaylovskoye that

Funeral for four of the Dyatlov hikers. (The fifth body, that
of Georgy Krivonishchenko, was buried separately.) Sverdlovsk,
March 9, 1959.

Mourners at the funeral for four of the Dyatlov hikers,
Sverdlovsk, March 9, 1959.

morning made the line between road and burial ground indistinguishable. "There were more than a thousand people flooding our neighborhood," Kuntsevich recalls. The boy had never seen such a gathering in his life, and his curiosity compelled him to leave the apartment and join the grieving masses below. The experience proved to be a life-altering one for Kuntsevich. He hadn't known any of the hikers, but he had been well aware of their disappearance and the subsequent search. His older brothers, Georgy and Eduard, were both UPI students at the time and were themselves outdoor enthusiasts. The tragedy seemed very close to the twelve-year-old boy, and not just because his family lived across the street from the cemetery.

Though Kuntsevich was young, he says he could recognize Soviet police when he saw them. He remembers seeing that day several men in civilian clothing paying close attention to the funeral crowd, but not to the service itself. "I am positive they were KGB, put there to monitor the events of the day." It wasn't long after Kuntsevich made his way across the street to the cemetery that the caskets were covered, lowered into the ground and buried. Afterward, someone stepped forward to recite a poem by Andrey Vostryakov:

Stand here shoulder to shoulder,
Touch the guitar strings gently,
Let the song be echoed
By mountains, wind and snow.

May the sorrowful ode
Remind us of young comrades,
Those who ran but couldn't
Escape a cruel fate.

Ripped was a side of the canvas,
Flapping in raging blizzards,
Letting frost and misfortune
Commit their deadly deed;

In their final struggle—
Hardy though they were,
Bravely though they battled—
Surrender to death they did.

Sleep, our dear souls,
Sleep, dear Igor and Zina,
Sleep, their fellow tourists,
Final shall be your sleep.

That gloomy mountain won't
Disturb your sleep any longer,
But under its fateful shadow
Your songs alive we'll keep.

Georgy Krivonishchenko was buried the following day, three miles west from where his friends lay, in a cemetery behind an Orthodox church on Repin Street. The Ivanovskoye Cemetery sat directly opposite the Central Stadium, a newly-built sports arena. A week earlier, the stadium had been teeming with fans attending the World All-Round Speed Skating Championships for Women, a first for the stadium and the city. But on March 10, the streets were quiet. Even with the gathering for Georgy's funeral, only a fraction of the previous day's mourners were in attendance.

After the funerals, many friends and relatives of the deceased began to explore alternate explanations for both the hikers' deaths and the authorities' odd behavior. The day after Georgy's burial, those who had attended the service gathered at the family's Sverdlovsk apartment. Georgy's father, Aleksey Krivonishchenko, later testified that the gathering included two hikers, who told him of their excursion into the northern Urals earlier that year, around the same time as the Dyatlov group's trip. These hikers told Krivonishchenko that on February 1, the same night his son died, they were one of two hiking groups who had witnessed a strange occurrence in the sky over the Ural Mountains, in the area around Otorten. "They saw a strange phenomenon in the evening to the north from their locations: the extremely bright light of some rocket," Krivonishchenko remembered. "The light was so bright that even those hikers who were preparing to sleep in tents went out to look at it. For some time, the sound of strong thunder came from afar."

Krivonishchenko didn't give the names of the hikers in his testimony of April 14, but it is possible he was speaking of a group led by a teacher named Shumkov, who claimed to have witnessed rockets over Chistop Mountain in early February, 25 miles south of the hikers' location. There were similar stories told by other hiking groups who were in the area from early- to mid- February. One of the most detailed accounts came from local hikers and search volunteers Georgy Atmanaki and Vladimir Shavkunov, who spoke of seeing "orbs" in the sky over the northern Urals on February 17. In Atmanaki's testimony to investigators, he stated that he and Shavkunov had woken at six in the morning to make breakfast for the group. As they were preparing the meal over a fire, he saw a strange white spot in the sky that he supposed at first to be the moon. But when he pointed it out to Shavkunov, his companion said that it couldn't be the moon because there was no moon that morning, and that if there had been, it would have been on the other side of the sky. "At that moment, a spark lit in the center of the spot," Atmanaki remembered. "It burned for several seconds steadily, then grew in size and flew swiftly west." Atmanaki said the sighting, which initially seemed a curiosity, grew more terrifying as it played out over the next minute and a half. "My personal feeling was that some celestial body was falling our way, but when it grew so large, I thought that some planet was coming in contact with Earth and that they would collide and Earth would perish."

Atmanaki's group wasn't alone. The Ivdel prosecutor's office brought in several witnesses who reported similar sightings the morning of February 17. Prison guards posted in the area described a slow-moving orb that "pulsed" in the sky, moving from south to north, and lasting anywhere from eight to fifteen minutes.

But how did strange phenomena in the February sky relate to the hikers' fates? The sister of Alexander Kolevatov suggested in her testimony that the answer might be found in the bodies themselves. "I was present at the funeral of all hikers," Rimma Kolevatova said. "Why did they have such brown skin on their faces and hands?" She went on to draw a connection between the hikers fleeing the tent in panic and the recent unexplained incidents in the sky over the Urals. "A group of hikers from the geographical faculty was at Chistop Mountain and (according to the witnesses) they saw some fire orbs on the same days, in the first days of February in the direction of Otorten Mountain. The same fire orbs were noticed later as well. Why is that? Could they have caused the death of the group?"

By the time the first hikers had been buried, the "orb" accounts and their attendant theories had infiltrated Lev Ivanov's investigation. The overwhelming number of witnesses who came forth to describe bizarre lights seen in the vicinity of Otorten Mountain—and to link the phenomenon back to the hikers' demise—made it difficult for the prosecutor's office to ignore this angle. It also made it more difficult for Ivanov and his crew to arrive at acceptable answers for the hikers' families. At some point in mid-March, a new piece of evidence emerged that would only bolster the theories of those who felt the orbs had something to do with the fate of the Dyatlov group. That evidence was in the final photographs taken by the hikers before they died.

★

22

2012

AROUND 4:30 AM, I WAS GENTLY SHAKEN AWAKE BY
Kuntsevich. Our transport had arrived in the Mansi village of Ushma,
the closest we could come to spending the night as the hikers had
at Sector 41. As I stumbled from the van into twenty-below-zero
weather, Kuntsevich motioned me toward a structure about 100
feet away, instructing me to wait there until the van was unpacked.

The headlights from our vehicle illuminated my way to a log
cabin, and I opened a flapping door and entered a dim anteroom
of sorts. There was another hanging curtain of heavy fabric in front
of me, evidently to block the draft. I pushed through it into a still
darker room. I had no flashlight on me and my cell phone had long
since died, so there was nothing I could do but wait until my pupils
adjusted. Suddenly a deep growl issued from the darkness in front of
me. I froze. The animal growled again, closer this time. But before
I could casually back myself toward the door, I heard a man's voice
shout commands at the animal; and the growling stopped. He spoke
again, clearly in my direction. I flipped through my mental phrase
book, and came up with "*Priviet Da?*" or "Hello, yes?"

There was a silence as the man evidently gathered that I was
a foreigner. The dog growled again, louder this time. Finally the
man asked, "*Amerikanski*"?

"*Da*," I managed to blurt out.

Finally, another few minutes passed in dark silence until I heard the footsteps of my team approaching from outside. Flashes from their headlamps illuminated parts of the room. I caught sight of a figure sitting on a cot, and a medium-sized dog at his side. With another flash of the headlamps, I noted the butt end of a shotgun sticking out from beneath the cot. Kuntsevich entered the room, followed by the others. The dog eventually stopped growling, but watched the intruders nervously. Kuntsevich said something to in Russian the strange man before ushering me over to a second cot. I noticed that it was the only other bed in the room and that the others were starting to spread their sleeping bags out on the floor. When I insisted on taking the floor, my three companions flatly refused. Too tired to argue, I unrolled my sleeping bag onto the metal cot and removed my boots. Then I curled up in my sleeping bag and drifted to sleep.

A DEEP, SPLITTING *CRACK!* FORCED ME AWAKE. I HAD TO switch on my headlamp in order to see anything. Borzenkov was on the floor asleep, still snug in his Technicolor snowsuit, with Voroshchuk sleeping beside him. The noise had come from the direction of Kuntsevich, who was standing near a rudimentary cement-brick stove and was bringing an ax down on a wedge of wood. I was happy to see someone preparing a fire, as I had never experienced a morning so miserably cold.

The structure was a one-room cabin in the style of nearly every home I'd seen pictured in this part of Russia. There was no running water, and therefore no bathroom, kitchen or basin. The walls were exposed logs and, from what I'd seen of the hikers' photos, similar to those of the Sector 41 cabins. The hikers must have awoken to a very similar view on their final morning in civilization.

Sleeping on a cot opposite me was our host, who I assumed to be the Mansi owner of the cabin. Lying across him was his dog, a German shepherd—the same breed that had been used during the search for the hikers. I was reminded of how the search dogs had slept in the tents with the volunteers each night. But the trade-off for their warmth had been the smell of wet fur, of which Ivanov had later complained to his family. This shepherd was now serving the same purpose, as a foul-smelling but affectionate electric blanket.

After Kuntsevich set fire to some kindling with a butane torch, he boiled a kettle of water. Borzenkov rose from the cold floor, presumably roused by the aroma of the instant coffee Kuntsevich had been preparing. He held out his hands for a mugful and took appreciative gulps.

The man and his dog awoke soon after, each stretching on the cot. He produced a large glass jar of what looked like stewed tomatoes, half slurped, half chewed the contents, and chased the mixture with swigs of vodka. The man and Kuntsevich exchanged a few words, but otherwise, things seemed to be business as usual. He put on his Valenki boots, threw a heavy jacket over his T-shirt and stepped out into the snow. I observed him through the window. He woke himself up with what I have since dubbed a "Russian snow bath." He removed his jacket and began by grabbing a handful of snow and rubbing it on his underarms, chest, neck and face. After a few deep breaths and invigorating chest pounds, he returned to the cabin.

After I finished my coffee, I put on my boots and stepped outside myself. The stillness of Ushma was otherworldly. Ivdel had been quiet, but at that moment, there was a silence to this native village that I had never experienced anywhere. I took in a sharp lungful of air. Then I stooped down and grabbed a handful of snow and stuck it beneath my clothing, attempting to replicate the snow bath. I braced for the shock of snow on my skin, but it was surprisingly pleasant and invigorating. Finally, with no one watching, I gave my chest a vigorous pounding. When I walked back into the cabin, I was greeted with a nod of comradeship, immediately realizing they'd witnessed my entire routine through the small front window. It seemed that I'd earned the man's approval and he motioned toward me. His name was Oleg. Through Voroshchuk, he apologized for the lack of a proper welcome the night before and for his dog. He had been in a drunken sleep when we arrived, and from his perspective an intruder had busted into his room unannounced. It turned out Kuntsevich, who arranged our stay in Ushma, failed to mention to Oleg that he would be traveling with an American. Kuntsevich also failed to mention to me—until months later, after I'd returned home—that Oleg was not a Mansi, as I had assumed given the location and rustic nature of our accommodations. He was, in fact, a thirty-year-old Russian who worked in rescue services in Ivdel. Staying in a freezing cabin with his dog in one of the more remote areas of Russia had evidently been Oleg's idea of a vacation.

AS WE ATE BREAKFAST FROM A CAN, MY COMPANIONS AND I discussed with our host our plans for getting to Holatchahl mountain. Voroshchuk translated only fragments of the conversation, but from what I could understand, there were potential weather problems on the pass. As we had all agreed to let Kuntsevich call the shots, only he would be able to give us the green light. Kuntsevich knew my determination to make the trip, but he would make the call.

As Oleg and the other three continued to weigh the risks of leaving that morning, I took the opportunity to step outside again and take in the village. Though it was mostly cloudy, some sunlight filtered through the evergreens and onto the snowy roofs of Ushma. A few of the cabins had smoke issuing from their chimneys, and I took a deep breath, pulling the smell of pine and burning firewood into my lungs. I learned later from a local Mansi man who visited our cabin that there were thirty villagers living here, mostly families, in about a dozen cabins. The Mansi here lived simply, supplementing government subsidies with subsistence farming and the sale from sable furs, the hunting of which is regulated by the government.

Not unlike the plight of Native Americans, who were forced from their lands during Manifest Destiny in the United States, the Mansi have been confined to smaller and smaller areas of land, mostly remote regions of the Ural Mountains. Today, they are represented in small villages such as Ushma, as well as settlements on the North Sosva and Ob Rivers. While census data has indicated a slow increase in the number of people claiming Mansi ethnicity (from 5,179 in 1926 to 12,269 in 2010), there are estimated to be fewer than a thousand who still speak the language, which suggests that it could be bound for extinction.

It took me less than thirty minutes to traverse the entire village over boot-trodden paths and through waist-deep snow. As I headed back to Oleg's cabin, I spotted something 100 yards in the distance. It was a large wooden bridge that spanned the frozen Auspiya River—the same river along which the Dyatlov group had skied over a half a century before.

★

23

WHEN INVESTIGATORS DEVELOPED THE FILM FROM THE Dyatlov group's cameras, the negatives revealed nothing out of the ordinary, at least not at first glance. The rolls from the three Zorki cameras belonging to Igor, Rustik and Georgy totaled eighty-eight exposures taken over nine days. They were images one would expect from such a trip—ten young people enjoying each other's company over winter break. Some of the shots were candid, capturing an arbitrary moment of preparation or rest. Others documented a charming vista, settlement or the locals encountered along the way. And then there were shots that were just silly, with the group striking comic poses in various combinations. About halfway into the rolls are the final images of Yuri Yudin in the company of his friends. He was in great pain at this point in the trip, pain that was forcing him to turn back, yet he smiled brightly in the direction of the photographer as he hugged his friends good-bye.

It was the final exposure on Georgy's camera that would continue to puzzle followers of the case. The image was dark, as if shot at night or in an enclosed space, but the camera was aimed toward an indistinct light source that dominated the left side of the frame. If the investigators in Sverdlovsk knew anything about photography, they would have quickly identified the octagonal circle of light at the center of the frame as a lens flare. But the

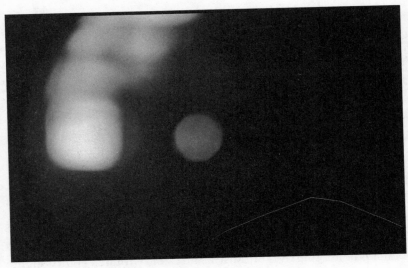

Last exposure on Georgy's camera, 1959.

large smear of light running up and off frame was mystifying, and would stoke half a century's speculation as to what happened in the hikers' final hours of life.

This last exposure failed to clear up anything about the hikers' fate and, if anything, had only confused those looking for answers. In 1990, decades after the close of the case, Lev Ivanov wrote that exposures taken by hikers gave him "abundant information based on negative density, film speed . . . and aperture and exposure settings" but that it did not "answer the main question—what was the reason of escape from the tent."

But according to Vladislav Karelin, one of the search volunteers who became closely involved with the investigation, Ivanov didn't need photographs—enigmatic or otherwise—to tell him that there was more to the case than some hikers running up against bad weather. The prosecutor had already been exploring the possibility that they had not died as a result of the elements.

In an interview Karelin gave to Russian author Anatoly Gushchin for his 2009 book *Murder at the Mountain of the Dead*, he said: "[I]n the first days of the investigation Ivanov reiterated that the students had died not of natural causes, and it had been a murder."

Because Karelin had been both intimately involved with the search, and also a member of the hiking group that had witnessed "fire orbs" in the sky on February 17, he was brought in for questioning by Ivanov in April. In the conclusion of his testimony, Karelin supported the prosecutor's murder angle. He conceded that there had been no evidence of a human assault outside the hikers' tent, but he told investigators that the only thing that could have scared them into leaving their tent without proper clothing would have been "a group of a dozen armed men." But Karelin retracted this statement years later in his interview with Gushchin: "I should say that this line appeared in my witness report owing to Lev Ivanov himself. He imposed it on me by asking a provocative question and then demanded to write it down in the report." How Ivanov imposed the theory upon him, Karelin doesn't elaborate.

In mid-March, Ivanov was called away to Moscow for reasons that he would not disclose to others in his office. Upon his return, Karelin and others noticed a pronounced change in his demeanor. "[W]e could not recognize him when he returned," Karelin said years later. "He didn't mention murder or spheres anymore. And he'd often advise us to 'hold our tongues.'"

In a 1990 letter to the *Leninsky Put* newspaper, Ivanov revealed that the regional Communist Party committee had instructed him not to pursue the connection between the strange lights in the sky and the hikers' deaths. He wrote that during the Cold War, "Such topics were prohibited in order to prevent the slightest possibility of disclosing data on missile and nuclear techniques." If Ivanov had up to that point been entertaining his own theories of murder and UFOs, he was told to set those theories aside for the good of his country.

★

THROUGHOUT MARCH AND APRIL THE SEARCH CONTINUES in the mountains for the remaining hikers — Lyuda Dubinina, Sasha Zolotaryov, Alexander Kolevatov and Kolya Thibault-Brignoles. The radiograms from this period reveal that the searchers concentrated their efforts on an ever-widening radius beyond the cedar tree where the first bodies had been found. By the end of April, the search effort has been operating for more than two months, and signs of wear are showing in the volunteers. There are repeated radiograms sent to Ivdel requesting the usual mood-elevating provisions of coffee and cigarettes. But these are meager comforts in the face of daily battles with lashing winds, deep snow and no hope for a happy ending. In early March, one volunteer slips off his skis and onto an exposed rock, resulting in a knee injury that swells over the next few days. When his condition worsens, he is evacuated by helicopter. But the snow is so deep on the pass that the volunteers have to throw one hundred buckets of water onto the snow to create a helipad.

On May 3, the Mansi searcher Stepan Kurikov comes across some unusual branches just under the snow in a ravine near the cedar tree. The branches appear to have been cut by a knife. Colonel Georgy Ortyukov, who is by that point overseeing the search operations, orders immediate probing of the area surrounding the branches.

On the first day of probing, about six yards away from the branches, a volunteer discovers a piece of clothing at the end of his metal probe. With shovels, he and his team dig a large hole above the creek bed, a cavity that will eventually reach a depth of 8 feet and an area of 100 square feet. The digging proceeds in fits and starts until the volunteers hit upon something solid. Realizing it is only a tree trunk, they move to a different spot and begin again.

Later that day, they hit upon a cache of clothing. What is odd about the articles is that they are abandoned in the snow, not attached to a person. Stranger still, some of the clothing looks to have been cut or shredded. There is a crumpled gray Chinese woolen vest turned inside out, knitted trousers, a brown woolen sweater with lilac thread, a right trouser leg and a bandage one yard long. The more Ortyukov and his men dig, the closer they come to the creek bed, which means, by the second day, that the men are digging through a combination of snow and slush. The second day of excavation reveals yet more clothing: black cotton sports trousers with the right leg missing—presumably the other half from the previous day's trousers—and half of a woman's sweater, belonging to Dubinina.

On the second evening, the men's shovels hit upon a body. It is clearly a man, though the decomposition from the water is such that the face is unrecognizable. He is wearing a gray sweater and, strangely, two wristwatches. The men continue to dig, soon uncovering three more bodies lying nearby. Lyuda's is the only identifiable one of the four. She is dressed in a cap, a yellow undershirt, two sweaters, brown ski trousers and two socks on one foot. The other foot is wrapped in a torn sweater. Her head is pointed upstream, while the three men are oriented toward the center of the stream. Two of the men are found in a position of embrace, in what appears to be a desperate attempt to conserve warmth.

When Lev Ivanov hears of the discovery, he flies to the mountains to assess the condition of the bodies, arriving on either May 5 or 6. The bodies, which have been lying in a soup of melting snow and creek water, are at various stages of decay. The volunteers have pulled them out of the slush at the bottom of the pit and have wrapped them in a tarpaulin to slow further decomposition. Ivanov notes that the body parts that have managed to avoid the water are mostly intact, but the flesh that was lying in the direct stream of

Volunteer Boris Suvorov stands with the hikers' clothing and a bed of twigs found beneath the snow, May 3, 1959.

The bodies of the last of the four hikers are pulled from a ravine, May 5, 1959. Colonel Georgy Ortyukov is pictured in the middle of frame with striped hat.

melting snow has succumbed to the water's microbes. The bodies need to be flown to Ivdel without delay, but the helicopter Ivanov himself flew in on has since left the area. Ivanov sends a radiogram to Ivdel stressing the urgency of the situation:

```
IF  THEY  ARE  NOT  EVACUATED  TOMORROW  THEY'LL
    DECOMPOSE.
```

Burying the bodies on the spot is out of the question, of course, and not just because their families will be robbed of a respectable burial. The last four hikers are the missing link in the story of what happened on the night of February 1. If their bodies are not immediately transported to Ivdel for a proper autopsy, Ivanov knows it will be a disastrous setback from which his investigation may not recover.

★

24

BY THE TIME I FINISHED MY TOUR OF USHMA, A LIGHT snow had begun to fall. I returned to the cabin to find my companions still discussing the weather. The consensus seemed to be that a storm was headed our direction, but the group was divided on whether or not one would strike us on the pass. Kuntsevich had, in any case, given his consent for the day's travel, though with some provisos. First, he was electing to stay behind as a point of contact in the village in case something were to happen to us on our journey. Second, we were to ride snowmobiles most of the way, at least to the Dyatlov incident's unofficial shrine, Boot Rock. And finally, we would not be camping on Holatchahl mountain, but would instead be returning to the village that night. At the mention of these last two conditions, I started to protest, but Kuntsevich was in no mood for discussion on the subject. It would be foolish in this weather, he insisted, to attempt the entire 45-mile trek along the river on foot, let alone contemplate spending more than one day out there.

But was the weather really any more dangerous than when the hikers had set out in the winter of 1959? Wasn't that the very point—to set up camp on the slope of Holatchahl, just as they had? Perhaps Kuntsevich was simply trying to save us from spending the night in dangerous, avalanche-prone territory. Snowmobiles, after all, were notorious for disrupting precarious snowdrifts and burying riders who refused to heed the warnings. Why tempt fate by spending the night beneath unsettled snow? My plans to shadow the hikers' exact movements were being checked at each turn, but in the chain of command, Kuntsevich had final say.

I was dismayed we wouldn't be making the trip in the same fashion as the hikers had—with skis strapped to our boots—but once our three snowmobiles had arrived, complete with three drivers, my objections fell away. Having never ridden a snowmobile, I found the entire prospect thrilling, and after climbing on behind my Russian driver, we were off on our terrestrial jet skis. But as we headed northwest from Ushma along the Lozva River, the hazards of our chosen mode of travel became quickly apparent. Driving on the frozen river itself was most efficient, but when the ice cracked beneath us, we quickly maneuvered to the bank. None of us was prepared for the roughness of the terrain: branches flying in our faces, rocks hidden beneath snow, and craters lying in ambush. Just staying on the vehicle required my intense concentration and there was little time to appreciate the landscape or to chat with my companions. The first hour passed without incident, but by the end of the second hour, our drivers had each wiped out more than once. There was an art to wiping out; the moment you sensed the snowmobile was about to tip over, you had to bail before the vehicle landed on top of you or on one of your limbs. I didn't need to be told more than once that breaking a bone out here would be bad news.

For 40 miles, there was nothing but the hum of the engines and the dark mass of the woods on either side of us. If there was ever an archetypal wood for Russian fairy tales (or nightmares), this was it. Then suddenly, into our sixth hour of travel, the trees stopped, and we entered an endless moonscape of snow. It might well have been the lunar surface if not for the occasional tree—that is, if you can call a dwarf pine that doesn't extend past one's knees a tree. We continued on in this nearly featureless topography, and about half an hour later, after we crested a small hill, a mottled black-and-gray shape seemed to rise out of the snow. As we drew closer, I recognized it as Boot Rock—a formation that did, in fact, resemble a hiking boot, if a severely mistreated one. The 30-foot-high jagged stone seemed an unlikely blemish upon the barren tundra, as if it had either been dropped from above or thrust up by a subterranean force.

It seemed wrong to ride up alongside the landmark, so after stopping at a respectful distance, the drivers turned off the engines and we headed to the rock on foot. For the families and friends of the Dyatlov hikers, and for followers of the case, Boot Rock has become a place of pilgrimage, at least during the warmer months when the rock is more accessible. Boot Rock has earned this sanctified distinction not because the hikers came here themselves, but because the search teams, who found themselves nearly a mile away from base camp, had taken shelter here from the February winds and snowfall. The rock had also served as a temporary grave marker for the bodies of the Dyatlov group, which had been stored here until they could be transported to Ivdel by helicopter.

I looked up to see a metal structure resembling a fez crowning the top of the rock, with a star perched on top of it. The 1959 search party had erected the ornament in order to better see the rock from a distance. On the far side of the rock, about six feet above the ground, we found the bronze plaque commemorating the Dyatlov party. In 1964, five years after the hikers' burial, Kuntsevich and his brothers had helped conceive of and mount the plaque for a special ceremony. Though Yuri Yudin hadn't made it to the mountains in 1959, he managed the trek to Boot Rock that summer to observe the five-year anniversary of the tragedy.

Friends, take off your hats
In front of this granite rock.
Guys, we won't let you go . . .
We keep warming up your souls,
Which are staying forever
In these mountains . . .

★

AS I CIRCLED THE ROCK, SEARCHING FOR EVIDENCE OF previous visitors, I came upon a tan Stetson tucked under a natural shelf about four feet above the ground. I lifted the hat to find a cache of notes, letters and poems dedicated to the Dyatlov group, most of them severely yellowed. Over the last fifty years , summer hikers had placed these items here out of the elements, like a time capsule, or a message in a bottle to others who managed the journey. There were rolled up bits of paper tucked into crevices, not unlike the notes in Jerusalem's Western Wall — and as much as I longed to read them, I dared not test their fragility. Also inside the recess were photographs of the hikers, many of them in their final days. There was an 8 x 10 laminated photo of Igor, one that was among my favorite likenesses of him. Igor is featured in close-up, dusted with snow and smiling rakishly for the camera. It is one of the few photographs in which the Dyatlov group leader appears unabashedly playful.

To celebrate our arrival at our penultimate stop, one of our snowmobile drivers pulled a flask from his jacket and proposed a toast. Then Borzenkov, Voroshchuk, the three snowmobilers and I took a swig. The drink instantly warmed my insides and I found a renewed strength to push onward to our final stop — the location of the hikers' tent, which was still a mile away. The landscape from that point became too steep to continue on our snowmobiles, so we left the vehicles — along with their drivers — at the rock and set out on foot. But as the effects of the vodka quickly wore off, and as snow flurries began to swarm around us, our uphill climb slowed. The ground beneath the snow was deceptively treacherous, with jagged rocks and cavities testing our balance at every step. And worse, I could feel my feet beginning to sweat, a curious sensation considering that the first three toes on my right foot were growing

numb with cold. My only guess was that my boots were not ventilat-
ing properly, and the more I perspired, the more my toes began to
stick together with frozen sweat. I couldn't imagine what I would
be experiencing now had we not taken the snowmobiles most of the
way. I marveled at the stamina of the young people who had come
through here five decades ago in worse weather and with inferior
outerwear. I stopped for a moment to rub the top of my right boot,
but Borzenkov reminded me to keep moving.

After about thirty minutes of climbing, I heard a shout behind
me and turned to see Borzenkov sliding down the slope. There was
nothing the rest of us could do but hope his momentum slowed or
that he caught hold of something. After what must have been at least
30 feet, he somehow stopped himself on some rocks protruding from
the snow. Thankfully, the rocks were not sharp enough to injure him,
and he slowly fought his way back to us. Our trek up the slope was
arduous, and consumed much of our remaining daylight and energy.

Once we got to a level stopping point, I asked Borzenkov how
close we were to the tent site. He said we must be nearing it, but
that it was virtually impossible to know until he spotted specific
indicators in the landscape. I could see that he was getting frus-
trated, but then with everything around us starting to look the same,
why wouldn't he? I found it incredible that the search volunteers
in 1959 had found the tent at all.

As we stopped to catch our breath again, Borzenkov pointed
ahead and off to the right to a vast assemblage of cedar trees
standing about a mile away. From this vantage point, the cedars
were merely an inky splotch against the snow and sky. This, he
explained, was where a few of the hikers had built a small fire after
initially leaving the tent. The site, of course, wasn't only where the
hikers made a fire; it was also where Yuri Doroshenko and Georgy
Krivonishchenko had died.

The sun was falling rapidly toward the horizon as we neared the
location of the tent an hour later. I worried not that we wouldn't

Vladimir Borzenkov (left) and the author on Holatchahl
mountain, February 2012.

have enough daylight to find our way back to Ushma—something
that, in retrospect, should have concerned me—but that it would be
too dark to see the site of the hikers' campsite clearly. Borzenkov
suddenly stopped to tell us that by his estimates we were nearing
the tent site. Not far off, I spotted the man-made landmark that
Kuntsevich had placed four years ago, a steel pole sticking out of
the snow that indicated where the tent had once stood. As I started
to move confidently toward the pole, Borzenkov confided to me
that Kuntsevich's marker was inaccurate. He instead pointed to
another spot about 1,000 feet away from the pole, explaining that
he had done precise measurements of the area. Using both GPS and
photogrammetry—the science of determining spatial measurements from photographs—he had arrived at this precise location.

When I reached the point Borzenkov had indicated, I turned
around, taking in 360 degrees of "Dead Mountain." The name
"Holatchahl" derives from the Finno-Ugric root "hoolat," meaning "dead"—Finno-Ugric being the larger linguistic grouping of
languages to which Mansi belongs. Despite a gloomy name that

invites a clear connection to be drawn to the Dyatlov tragedy, Mansi semantics experts believe the mountain to have been named for its lack of vegetation. In this meaning, "Mountain of the Dead," as some have come to call it, is incorrect. "Dead Mountain" is the proper translation, which certainly made sense to me—there was no life up here to speak of. I didn't find the slope particularly beautiful or inspiring, and for some reason, I found the bald dome of the summit difficult to look at.

In unspoken agreement, the three of us stood there on the slope of Holatchahl in silence, knowing that at the very least, this place deserved a certain respect for the nine who had once stood here. But as the biting wind swept down the slope, it created a shrill whistle—a sound both beautiful and terrifying.

After our moment of silence, I got to work examining the site of the tent and the surrounding area. The moment we had arrived on the slope, my mind had already been jumping to conclusions, but I tried to slow my thinking and examine the surroundings. To this end, I trudged along the slope to see how the snow would behave, and no snow fell or slid downward. I was surprised to see that the incline wasn't nearly as steep as I'd imagined. Borzenkov told me he had previously used GPS to calculate the angle of the slope. His data showed that it was extremely unlikely for a soft, slab or slush avalanche to have occurred. The slope's "run-out angle" — the angle that determines how far an avalanche will move—was 16 degrees from the top of the slope to the tent's location. At 16 degrees, it would be nearly impossible for an avalanche to travel half the distance of a football field over such a flat surface to reach the tent. The slope angle below the tent was 25 degrees, which would be steep enough to slide only in the rarest conditions. While standing on the mountain it occurred to me that even if an avalanche had happened here, in spite of the data, it would have been impossible for the hikers to get out of the tent before the snow hit them and their tent. At most, the hikers would have ten seconds before the snowpack hit the tent and carried it down the slope. But this theory would work only if the avalanche could travel such a great distance over a shallow surface, and if the tent were not found still standing with contents in place and if the hikers were not found over a mile away from their campsite. Not only did an avalanche here appear extremely unlikely; we found it difficult to believe that any of the Dyatlov hikers would have considered even the threat of an avalanche enough reason to abandon the tent.

Avalanche aside, there was another aspect of the case that had always puzzled me, but was only now hitting me with full force: I couldn't conceive of how the hikers could have left their tent improperly clothed—most without shoes—to walk almost a mile to the cedars along the horizon. It took us well over an hour to walk half a mile in these conditions, and we were equipped with warmer clothing and modern hiking gear. According to Borzenkov's analysis after studying weather records of the surrounding areas from February 1, 1959, the Dyatlov group would have faced strong winds of up to 40 miles per hour on their descent into the cedars. There had been a waning crescent moon of 33 percent on the night of February 1, which might have provided some light once it had risen. But even if the moon had not been obscured by clouds, it didn't rise until after four in the morning—four to six hours after it's believed the nine hikers left the tent. Our current conditions of minus twenty degrees Fahrenheit were close to those the Dyatlov group would have experienced in 1959. Combined with the aggressive winds and a wind chill estimated at forty below zero, the poorly clothed hikers would have had a maximum of six to eight hours to live. After the hikers reached the cedars, it would have been next to impossible to find the tent and return to it.

The combination of strong winds and subzero temperatures had clearly led to the hikers' deaths; that much was clear. But the case still boiled down to a single question: What, if not an avalanche, provoked the nine hikers to leave the sanctuary of their tent?

★

25

GETTING THE FOUR REMAINING BODIES DOWN FROM THE mountains and onto an examining table was not an easy task. By now the Dyatlov case's notoriety had spread through the Sverdlovsk region and beyond, as had all its attendant rumors and theories. It seemed that everyone in the region had his or her own idea as to what had happened to the hikers that night—speculation that ranged from Mansi killers and mysterious armed men, to experimental military aircraft and radioactive weapons. By spring, the suppositional winds were blowing in the direction of a military cover-up. One of the members of the search party who had been on the scene when the remaining bodies were found, had one such theory involving UFOs and temporary insanity. Nikolay Kuzminov spoke for many of those who had witnessed bizarre lights in the sky that winter. In a letter printed in Gushchin's *Murder at the Mountain of the Dead*, Kuzminov wrote: "I think that their death was caused by 'fire orbs,' which we saw one night too, followed by five to six minutes of mind confusion." In support of this, Kuzminov pointed out that the hikers had strayed from their tent like a bunch of "lunatics."

Lyuda Dubinina's own father, in his testimony from mid-April, weeks before his daughter's body was found, talked of a similar force affecting the hikers' senses. "I think a missile was launched from within the USSR," Alexander Dubinin said. "It all makes me think that they fled from the tent due to an explosion and emission near the height of 1,079 [yards] . . . which forced the hikers to run away from the tent and maybe it affected their condition, particularly their sight."

With all these theories in rampant circulation, Lev Ivanov may not have been too surprised when, after he requested an Air Force helicopter to transport the hikers' bodies, the pilot, Captain Gatezhenko, refused to let the bodies near his aircraft. Either Gatezhenko hadn't realized the nature of the mission when he agreed to it, or something about the tarpaulin-covered corpses gave him pause. Either way, when he arrived at the scene, he refused to carry out the task, informing Ivanov and Colonel Ortyukov that his chief wouldn't approve of the transportation of corpses without the proper vessel. He specifically requested zinc-lined coffins, which were sealed to prevent toxic or biological leakage.

Gatezhenko's refusal to carry the corpses without the proper coffins resulted in a heated argument with Colonel Ortyukov, and when the colonel failed to make any headway with the stubborn pilot, he fired off a radiogram to Ivdel. "It's disgraceful, I and fourteen other comrades brought corpses by hand to the helicopter," Ortyukov wrote to Comrade Prodanov, a member of the search efforts in Ivdel. "Despite my compelling requests, they didn't take the bodies aboard. As a Communist I'm shocked with the actions of crew and ask you to inform city committee of the Party and commander Colonel General Lelyushenko thereof." Ortyukov went on to explain that examination of the bodies on the spot was impossible, as the one forensic expert on the scene refused to perform an autopsy "due to the state of the bodies." Ortyukov sent a follow-up message later that day emphasizing the integrity of the tarps and requesting that the Air Force order the immediate evacuation of the corpses without special coffins. Prodanov replied he would try to persuade the Air Force, but added "they'll hardly agree to transport them without coffins." Prodanov's next radiogram was the final word on the subject: "Zinc-coated coffins ordered today, will be delivered tomorrow." The corpses would have to keep another day.

On May 8, four days after their discovery, the hikers' bodies were taken to the mortuary at Ivdel's central hospital for forensic examination.

★

WITH IVANOV PRESENT IN THE EXAMINATION ROOM, A Sverdlovsk forensic expert named B. A. Vozrozhdyonny set to work on finding out how the last four Dyatlov hikers had died. He had been present during the first five autopsies, though his colleague Ivan Laptev had actually performed them. Vozrozhdyonny had been anticipating—and no doubt dreading—this very summons all spring.

First on the examining table was twenty-four-year-old Alexander Kolevatov. Vozrozhdyonny began by cataloguing Kolevatov's abundant pieces of clothing, noting the conspicuous—though by now expected—lack of footwear. Though Kolevatov had gone out into the snow without his boots, no responsible outdoorsman is ever caught without matches—and he had a matchbox in one of his pockets, along with a packet of (now empty) painkillers. Kolevatov's ankle had also been bandaged, which indicated a previous hiking injury, though one apparently not serious enough to prevent his participation on the hike. The rest of the examination found nothing unusual about the body other than rigor mortis, livor mortis and the accompanying discoloration of the skin and organs, and Vozrozhdyonny concluded that Kolevatov had died of hypothermia, as had the first five hikers found. No surprise there.

With the first examination out of the way, Vozrozhdyonny and Ivanov might have expected that the three others had met the same fates. And, indeed, upon initial examination of thirty-seven-year-old Sasha Zolotaryov, things seemed to be progressing as the previous examination had. Zolotaryov was wearing generous layers of clothing, no shoes, and his skin and organs showed the same discoloration. One superficial difference was Zolotaryov's multiple tattoos. In addition to a tattoo of beets and the name Gena on his right arm and hand, his left arm revealed a five-pointed star and the number (or year) 1921. It was Zolotaryov's midsection that struck the forensic analyst as unusual: The right side of his chest had sustained serious injury, with five fractured ribs resulting in severe hemorrhaging. Vozrozhdyonny concluded that the fractures had been inflicted by a "large force" while the victim had been alive.

For twenty-three-year-old Kolya Thibault-Brignoles, Vozrozhdyonny found similar violent injuries, though this time the fractures were to the head. He concluded that Kolya had died of "impressed fracture of skull dome and base with abundant hemorrhage." He added that the injury had been sustained while the hiker had been alive by "effect of a large force."

The forensic expert's examination of Lyudmila Dubinina was the most alarming. The twenty-year-old's body had sustained massive thoracic damage, with internal hemorrhaging, including that of her right heart ventricle, plus fractures to nine of her ribs. Most disturbing, however, was that when Vozrozhdyonny examined the young woman's mouth, he saw that her tongue was missing. He offered no explanation in his report for this last detail, concluding only that, along with two of her companions, Lyuda's death could be classified as "violent."

But what exactly did "violent" suggest in this case? Had the violence been inflicted by a natural force or a human one? The May 9 autopsies failed to provide satisfactory answers to these questions, but Ivanov was determined to learn all he could about the hikers' final hours, ideally before their bodies were put in the ground.

The four funerals were scheduled for May 22, to be held at the military hospital in Sverdlovsk. Unlike the first five funerals, which had been conspicuously public, now only the families of the victims were permitted to attend.

In the meantime, speculation about the hikers' fates continued to circulate. On May 15, Ivanov brought in for questioning Vadim Brusnitsyn, a search volunteer, third-year UPI student and friend of the hikers. Why Ivanov was still bringing in witnesses at this late date is unclear, though he may well have been casting about for something that could make sense of the recent autopsies. Brusnitsyn told Ivanov that he didn't think there was anyone among the Dyatlov group who would have infected the others with unnecessary panic, and that something "unusual, unprecedented" must have compelled his friends to escape the tent. "Only a threat of death can make people run barefoot at night from the only warm shelter," he said. He went on to suggest that a strange phenomenon such as "light penetrating the tent walls," "a sound" or "gases" might have driven the hikers far from their tent.

All this speculation about extraordinary phenomena meant little, of course, without solid evidence. Ivanov knew that he needed more information to properly interpret the "violent" classification of the forensic expert. So four days before the funerals, Ivanov ordered radiological tests performed on the hikers' organ samples and clothing. The results of the tests, however, would not be available for another eleven days, after the hikers were buried.

On May 22, the Dubinin, Zolotaryov, Kolevatov and Thibault-Brignoles families gathered at the Sverdlovsk military hospital for a closed casket funeral. The families had requested open caskets, but Ivanov denied this request due to the advanced decomposition of the bodies. He later regretted this decision, as revealed only decades later in a 1990 interview with a Sverdlovsk journalist, S. Bogomolov. "I should be blamed a lot by their relatives. I didn't let them see the bodies of their children," Ivanov said. "I made the only exception for the father of Dubinina. I opened the coffin cover a bit to show that his daughter was dressed properly." The reaction of Alexander Dubinin might have vindicated the investigator's decision to keep the caskets closed. Dubinin was so horrified by the condition of his daughter's body that he fainted on the spot.

A week later, the radiation tests came back from the city's chief municipal radiologist, a man named Levashov. According to Levashov's report, the hikers' organs revealed the presence of the radioactive substance potassium-40. Though this might have seemed cause for alarm, Levashov quickly pointed out that separate samples taken from the victim of a fatal Sverdlovsk car crash revealed the same levels of potassium-40, suggesting that this was a naturally occurring isotope.

The radiation measurements of the hikers' clothing, however, was a different matter, and Levashov's own interpretation of the data is one of the central reasons the Dyatlov case has continued to spawn conspiracy theories some five decades later. Levashov stated that the Soviet Union's "sanitary standards" for beta-particle contamination were under 5,000 decays per minute per 23 square inches. If the hikers had been exposed to natural levels of radiation, why then was a brown sweater belonging to one of the hikers (probably Kolevatov or Lyuda) found to contain almost twice this number—9,900 decays per minute? According to Levashov, this level of contamination "exceeds standards for people working with radioactive substances." It turned out that the other pieces of clothing found on the hikers also measured at levels above the normal 5,000 decays per minute. And because the clothing had been sitting for days in melting snow and water, Levashov suggested that "one can suppose that the initial contamination was much higher." When the question was put to Levashov if the clothing could have become contaminated by radioactive substances under normal conditions, he said that this was impossible. "The clothes are contaminated either with radioactive dust from the atmosphere or by contact with radioactive substances. As I've said, this contamination exceeds standards for people working with radioactive substances."

But the radiation tests and their alarming implications would have no bearing on the active criminal case. Just one day before the radiation tests were to come back from the lab, Ivanov bowed to pressure from his regional superiors to terminate the criminal investigation, effective immediately. Though Ivanov did have the option to apply for a one-month extension, it would have been unusual to do so in a case in which the bodies had already been found. Additionally, applying for an extension would have put immense stress on Ivanov to produce conclusive new evidence within a month. And so on May 28, without being able to follow through on the tests that he himself had ordered, Ivanov closed the Dyatlov case, citing no particular cause for the hikers' deaths.

In the coming days, the hikers' families would become outraged by the lack of communication from the prosecutor's office. The parents of the victims were shown and told nothing, and probably had no idea even that radiation tests had been performed. Yuri Yudin remembers that the only decisive action the authorities took was to close the northern Ural Mountains to hikers for three years. (Hiking permits were denied. But given the remote nature of the terrain, people could still venture there at their own risk.) There were also the expected punishments doled out to various organization heads for their failure to prevent such a tragedy. UPI, for its part, dismissed the sports club director, Lev Gordo, for giving students leave to explore avalanche-prone areas of the Urals. The director of the university, N. Siunov, was officially reprimanded for failing to adequately oversee the sports club, as were Valery Ufimtsev and V. Korochkin at the municipal level. And, finally, Party secretary O. Zaostrovsky was reprimanded for his part in failing to police all the sports clubs, both university and city.

The case files, however, came to no conclusions about the night of February 1, avalanche or otherwise. Before Ivanov shut the casebook forever, he cited the cause of the hikers' deaths as "an unknown compelling force." For the next forty-plus years, the families and friends of the hikers would have nothing more than this cryptic summation to explain the secretive behavior of their government and the harrowing deaths of the people they had loved.

★

26

2013

BACK IN LOS ANGELES, IN WHAT HAD ONCE BEEN THE
garage of my house, I built something of a command center. In the
year since my return from Russia, I had struggled to make sense of
the evidence and investigative materials surrounding the Dyatlov
case. The focal point of the room was a wall of photographs I had
mounted to illustrate the progression of the hikers' journey and
the timeline of the investigative case.

What I had learned on my second trip to Russia was of immea-
surable value, but I had left the country without an answer—without
the answer. But then, of all those who have trekked to Holatchahl
mountain, why had I assumed I'd be the one to solve this puzzle?
Was it because I had gone in the middle of winter and had trudged
through knee-deep snow? Did I think that by retracing the hikers'
footsteps and standing on the slope where they had pitched their
tent, the answer would be handed to me?

My entire strategy thus far had been process of elimination, not
unlike the oft-quoted maxim of Sherlock Holmes: "When you have
eliminated the impossible, whatever remains, however improbable,
must be the truth." In that spirit, I had been able to eliminate the
following theories with a satisfying degree of certainty:

1. MANSI ATTACK. Though initially considered a viable angle
in the 1959 investigation, it was quickly discarded. At the time

of the incident the nearest Mansi settlement was 60 miles away. Besides, the Mansi tended to stay away from Holatchahl mountain; there was no hunting to be had on its bare face, nor did it hold any religious or sacred value to the group. Aside from there being zero evidence—physical or otherwise—of a native attack, such behavior is not in the nature of the Mansi: They are a historically peaceful people, a fact evident in their generous assistance from the beginning in the search efforts.

2. AVALANCHE. I had been able to judge the steepness of the slope for myself firsthand. In addition, measurements of the incline pointed to an avalanche in the area being unlikely, if not impossible. There are no records of an avalanche occurring on Holatchahl mountain—certainly not in the fifty-four years since the tragedy. Furthermore, investigators who had visited the slope in 1959—including Ivanov and Maslennikov—had not entertained an avalanche as a possibility, nor had they found any indications of one. After all, the tent had been found largely intact and secured to the ground. During my own research on the subject, I contacted Bruce Tremper, one of the foremost experts on avalanches in the United States. He is director of the Forest Service Utah Avalanche Center and author of *Staying Alive in Avalanche Terrain*. After reviewing the data, he concluded: "It is highly unlikely that an avalanche hit the hikers' tent or surrounding area." Given all of the above, it is surprising that the theory continues to have such staying power among skeptics.

3. HIGH WINDS. The hikers had been warned about dangerous winds on the pass, most notably by the Vizhay forester Ivan Rempel, who had told stories of locals being swept away. This was also an angle seriously considered by investigators at the time. The idea was that one or two persons outside the tent—those presumably wearing the cloth boot liners—had stepped outside, possibly to

urinate, when an overpowering wind took them by surprise. Their cries roused those inside the tent not only to jump outside to save them, but also to cut through the canvas in their haste. But this theory supposes that all the hikers would have flung themselves into the wind to save their friends, one by one, heedless of the dangers. This does not seem likely. One of the hikers would surely have put on a pair of shoes. The theory also requires the winds to have been powerful enough to blow all nine hikers off the face of the mountain, yet not strong enough to blow away the tent or Rustik's knit hat (which was securely on his head when he was found). According to Borzenkov's weather analysis, the winds had indeed been strong that night—up to 40 miles per hour—but they would not have reached destructive levels on the Beaufort wind scale, let alone anywhere near hurricane-force (74 mph and above). Of all the theories, this had initially struck me as the least improbable. But given the intelligence of Igor and his comrades, and the strength of the winds that night, I could now eliminate it with confidence.

4. ARMED MEN.   Despite all evidence to the contrary, the theory that a group of armed men—either Soviet military or escaped prisoners—led the hikers to their deaths is a stubborn one that has continued to plague the Dyatlov case. Although this scenario had been briefly considered by Lev Ivanov and his investigators—most notably after knife slashes at the back of the tent were discovered—it was largely dismissed after the cuts were determined to have been made from the inside of the tent. Additionally, only nine sets of footprints were found at the scene. There was no evidence, from tracks or otherwise, of visitors to the tent that night. And there were zero reports at the time of prisoners having escaped from any of the surrounding camps, the closest of which was over 50 miles away.

Claims that some of the hikers' belongings had gone missing are overstated. After examining the criminal case file, I found that the toy hedgehog Yudin believed to be missing had, in fact, been found among the hikers' belongings, though mistakenly catalogued with Rustik's things. The missing chocolate was most likely consumed by search volunteers upon discovery of the tent. In my interview with Boris Slobtsov, for instance, he confessed that he and Mikhail Sharavin, after locating the tent, had drunk the hikers' flask of medicinal alcohol.

To explain the forensic examiner's discovery of violent injuries on three of the hikers' bodies—including hemorrhaging, multiple rib fractures and a fractured skull—one needn't look farther than the ravine in which the bodies were found. The 24-foot-high precipice on one side of the ravine—at an incline between 50 and 60 degrees—would have given the four hikers who had happened upon it in the pitch darkness a nasty fall. Given that there were rocks at the bottom of the ravine, just a few inches beneath the snow, the resulting injuries would have been serious enough for Ivanov to compare the impact to "a large directional force, such as a car." Ivanov, however, was not a doctor or an expert in such injuries. Additionally, the forensic examiner's conclusion that three of the deaths had been "violent" is consistent with a lethal fall into the ravine.

Damage to Lyuda's tongue can be blamed on the natural decomposition process. One theory suggests that small animals got to her tongue, but because her body had been lying in melted snow, it is more likely that over several weeks, the microfauna in the water decomposed the fleshiest parts of her body.

5. WEAPONS TESTING.
- **Rocket tests/"Orbs."** He hadn't been able to say so publicly while he was investigating the case, but Lev Ivanov had believed the orb sightings of February 1959 to be connected to the hikers' deaths. After his retirement, in his 1990 interview with journalist S. Bogomolov, he revealed, "I can't tell for sure whether those orbs were weapons or not, but I'm

certain that they were directly related to the death of the hikers." That same year, in a lengthy letter to the *Leninsky Put* newspaper on November 22, he connected the orbs to the violent injuries of three of the hikers: "Someone wanted to intimidate people or show off power, and so they did so by killing three hikers. I know all details of this event and can say that only those who were inside the orbs know more than me. Whether there were 'people' inside that time or any time is yet unclear." Ivanov was reluctant to say whether or not he thought the "orbs" were a kind of weapon, preferring instead to talk in vague terms of "energy bundles unexplained by modern science." But elsewhere in the letter, he maintained that "the investigation showed that Dyatlov's case was not related to the military." With a Cold War going on, classified rocket launches would not have been unusual in 1959, and indeed there had been such tests in February and March of that year. But none would have affected the Dyatlov hikers on the night of February 1 and 2. In fact, there is no evidence of any unusual sightings on that night.

The purported "light orb" sightings of early February were more accurately seen midmonth. Hiker Georgy Atmanaki had originally told investigators he had seen the orbs during the first week of February. But his companion on the same trip, Vladislav Karelin, later confirmed the date was much later, February 17. This coincides with Ivdel witnesses who reported seeing lights in the sky on the same day. For many, including relatives of the hikers, it had been tempting to connect the midmonth sightings with the tragedy of February 1. The "orb" sightings of February 17 and March 31, as described by numerous witnesses, happened within minutes of corroborated rocket tests from the Baikonur testing site—otherwise known as the Soviet Missile and Space Station. Any other rocket tests in the Soviet Union during that period came from Heiss Island, an island in the northern archipelago of Franz Josef Land, which was over 1,200 miles away from where the hikers had set up camp. With the maximum flight range of these M-100 rockets being no more than 100 miles, I could eliminate rocket-related scenarios with certainty.

The final photo taken on Georgy's camera—featuring an unknown light source—has fueled much speculation about the hikers having encountered weapons testing or UFOs. I myself had been tempted to connect this photo to something the hikers had been trying to photograph in their final hours. I determined that the octagonal shape at the center is a flare resulting from the eight blades on the camera's aperture. Though the source of light is nearly impossible to determine, the lack of focus of the image, and the smear of the light source, is consistent with it having been taken accidentally—by the hikers or even possibly by the search party or the investigators.

- **Radiation-related tests.** The radiation that had been detected on the hikers' clothes is largely responsible for the idea that some weapon, potentially nuclear in nature, had exploded above or near the campsite and had forced the hikers from their tent—causing injury and affecting their vision. After the autopsies, two sets of the hikers' clothes tested two to three times higher than normal for radiation. I submitted these test results to Dr. Christopher Straus, associate professor of radiology at the University of Chicago Medical Center to find out if the original verdict would hold up. Dr. Straus was able to determine, upon first glance, that by today's scientific understanding of radiation levels, the beta particle decays cited in the criminal case for the hikers' clothing were nowhere near an abnormal range. They would have had to be 50 to

100 times the level detected to reach dangerous or alarmingly abnormal levels of radiation. The slight positive result in the hikers' clothing could easily be explained by environmental contaminants—for example, radiation from nuclear tests conducted that winter on the islands of Novaya Zemlya, 850 miles to the north of the hikers' location, could have found its way to the northern Urals through the atmosphere and water cycle. Additionally, the dark or "orange" color of the hikers' skin is more plausibly explained as a severe tan or sunburn, rather than exposure to radiation. Before becoming buried in snow, the bodies likely had lain out for many days. Even with no sun, UV rays would have penetrated the cloud cover. Dr. Reed Brozen, medical director of Dartmouth-Hitchcock Medical Center's Advanced Response Team, and an expert in wilderness medicine and hypothermia, explained to me that "with the altitude, UV light, and zero percent humidity, the bodies could have become mummified over time."

6. "IT'S CLASSIFIED." Many Dyatlov case enthusiasts—the Dyatlov Foundation's Yuri Kuntsevich among them—still believe the answer to the Dyatlov mystery lies in classified government documents that have yet to be released. However, the behavior of both Soviet and Russian officials hardly points to the existence of secret files. Per Soviet law, criminal case files were to be stored in the prosecutor's office for twenty-five years. If no appeals were filed for the case during that time, the entire case could be legally destroyed. The Soviet government had its chance to completely destroy the Dyatlov case files, but it chose not to. Despite the fact that there were no appeals filed for twenty-five years after the close of the case, the Sverdlovsk prosecutor's office chose to leave the case files intact in their archives. The files were later released in the late 1980s and early '90s, during glasnost. Considering that much of the Stalin archive was released during that time, thereby

revealing many incidents deeply embarrassing to the country's government—including the 1962 Novocherkassk massacre in which Soviet troops with machine guns mowed down a group of factory protesters—what would be so special about nine hikers dying in the northern Urals? Conspiracists will likely never give up on the theory of a government cover-up, but the idea that the Russian government is holding onto secret case files is implausible.

7. SPACE ALIENS, ETC.   There were, of course, those who would put forth interstellar visitation as the answer to Sherlock Holmes's "whatever remains, however improbable." But I was holding out hope that I could find an explanation that didn't involve extraterrestrials. I'm not saying I don't entertain the idea of life existing out there somewhere in the vast universe, but if one is going to fall back on malevolent alien visitors without backing it up with evidence, one may as well throw ghosts, the hand of God, and devious subterranean gnomes into the mix. Aliens were off the table.

I DON'T REMEMBER SHERLOCK HOLMES EVER MENTIONING what you are supposed to do when you've eliminated everything improbable, and nothing is left.

The *least improbable* answer still seemed to lie, if not in an avalanche, then in some sort of other natural occurrence. I'd been reading up on weather phenomena, in the hope I might discover something relevant to the case, something I'd managed to miss. I'd always enjoyed reading about bizarre weather events. When you grow up in Florida, a.k.a. "hurricane alley," obsessing about weather phenomena is a rite of passage. I had also been somewhat of a weather wonk as a teen, not because meteorology itself had initially interested me—my interest in forecasting grew out of my love of surfing. As any surfer knows, where there was intense weather off the coast, such as a hurricane or low-pressure system, there were also long-period ground swells that produced good waves.

Among the articles I had printed out related to weather was one particular piece I thought might be related to the topic of experimental weapons—infrasound weaponry in particular. It was a piece from a *Physics Today* issue from 2000. The piece in question—entitled "Atmospheric Infrasound"—was written by a Dr. Alfred J. Bedard, Jr. and Thomas M. Georges. I wasn't entirely sure what the title meant, though it intrigued me. The Bedard-Georges study examined the occurrence of sound waves that travel through the air at frequencies below those on the audible spectrum, frequencies referred to as *infrasound*. Infrasound is the opposite of ultrasound; it occurs below the threshold of human hearing at 20 hertz, while ultrasound frequencies fall above hearing at a threshold at 20,000 hertz.

A pioneer in the biological effects of infrasound was the Russian-born, French scientist Vladimir Gavreau, who discovered its impact on the body entirely by accident. During the 1960s, Gavreau and his laboratory assistants started experiencing inexplicable nausea, pain in their eardrums and shaking lab equipment—all with no apparent cause. When all chemical and airborne sources were ruled out, Gavreau eventually concluded that inaudible, low-frequency sounds waves were being generated by the motor of a large fan-and-duct system in the building where his lab was located. What initially started out as a subconscious irritation, soon became a scientific pursuit for Gavreau—but it was a difficult one for him to pursue, as no traditional microphone could pick up the frequencies, and exposing himself and his assistants to the infrasound resulted in severe illness, sometimes lasting days.

Gavreau determined that he and his assistants were suffering from the pressurized effects of infrasonic frequencies pulsing through their eardrums. These low-frequency waves can cause the eardrum to vibrate the hair cells of the inner ear. The effect of this is that, although the sound may not be "audible" to the casual listener, the excited hair cells in the inner ear send impulses to the brain—and this disconnect between apparent silence and the brain's receiving signals from the ear, can be extremely disruptive to the body.

I learned that man-made sources of infrasound were numerous—cooling and ventilation systems and wind farms being typical culprits—but these low-frequency waves also occurred in nature as by-products of earthquakes, landslides, meteors, storms and tornadoes. The Bedard-Georges study outlined and studied these infrasonic occurrences in nature; in particular, when winds of a certain speed encounter an obstructive landscape. I later learned that this naturally occurring infrasound could be devastating to humans, causing nausea, severe illness, psychological disturbances and even suicide—symptoms not unlike those theoretically produced by experimental infrasound weaponry.

I e-mailed Borzenkov about the avenues I had recently been exploring, hoping that my Google-translated text would convey the finer points of the Bedard-Georges article. I didn't expect to hear from him immediately. He had recently fallen ill, and his treatment limited his ability to research and write as effortlessly as he used to. Despite my repeated concerns and questions about his health, Borzenkov would not reveal the nature of his illness—how severe it might be, for example, or whether he had years or months to live. I knew by now that this was the Russian way. If his illness had not affected his ability to respond to my e-mails, he probably wouldn't have divulged his health problems to me at all.

WHEN BORZENKOV REPLIED SEVERAL DAYS LATER, I COULD sense his frustration even through the muddled translation. He had already been looking into the naturally occurring version of the infrasound phenomenon. Had I not read his e-mails on the subject? I looked back over his previous messages to me about infrasound, and how he had speculated that "infrasound had caused the hikers to leave the tent," but the poorly translated text had not communicated the distinction he had evidently been making between wind-generated and weapon-generated infrasound. His new e-mail went on to say that he was in touch with infrasound experts in Russia—at Lomonosov State University—and the emerging theory was that Boot Rock had been responsible for creating low-frequency sound waves that had driven the hikers from their tent. I conjured up the shape of the rock in my mind, imagining fierce winds whipping past its jagged edges, hurtling infrasound waves toward the vulnerable tent on the slope. Could this really be the theory I was looking for?

My miscommunication with Borzenkov was not surprising—trying to explain a very complex scientific phenomenon is difficult enough without language complications. I decided that in order to avoid further confusion caused by the language barrier, I needed to get in touch with an infrasound expert who spoke English, preferably in the United States.

Further research confirmed that Dr. Bedard, co-author of the *Physics Today* paper, was indeed the authority in the field I needed to speak with. His area of expertise in the detection of naturally occurring infrasound, particularly in mountainous regions, could not have been better. His knowledge in the field of meteorology and atmospheric phenomena had resulted in his one hundred publications, two books, five patents, and over thirty detection devices. Meeting him wouldn't require my flying overseas, either. He was senior scientist and infrasonics group leader at the National Oceanic and Atmospheric Administration (or NOAA) in Boulder, Colorado—only a few hours' plane ride away.

Although it wasn't easy to reach Dr. Bedard, when I finally got him on the phone and filled out the whole story, he confessed that while he had never heard of the Dyatlov Pass incident, several of his

Russian colleagues at NOAA were familiar with the tragedy. He had only just learned how famous the incident was to most Russians. If I came to Boulder, Dr. Bedard said, he and his team could meet with me to discuss the case further. I hung up the phone, both thrilled and a little intimidated. I was meeting with a team of atmospheric physicists, and I had better come prepared.

CREATED UNDER PRESIDENT RICHARD NIXON, AND FALLING under the jurisdiction of the Department of Commerce, NOAA was the first agency in the country committed solely to atmospheric sciences; in fact, it was an aggregate of three preexisting agencies: the US Coast and Geodetic Survey, the Weather Bureau and the Bureau of Commercial Fisheries. In his statement to Congress in 1970, Nixon called for a new agency "for better protection of life and property from natural hazards . . . for a better understanding of the total environment . . . [and] for exploration and development leading to the intelligent use of our marine resources." Currently, over 12,500 employees work for NOAA across the country and worldwide, with fewer than one thousand of those stationed at NOAA Boulder.

I arrived at the NOAA center, a federal building, on a morning in mid-February. The security was intense and incredibly thorough. I'd had to forward all my personal information for clearance before I even booked my flight, and then there were three separate security stops on the grounds themselves. After I stopped my rental car at the first station, the guards checked my ID, ran my backpack through a security machine and examined my Dictaphone. I was given a badge, which read under my name, "Escort Required." Next, I was ushered through an airport-style security machine, before arriving at a security gate where another set of guards checked my clearance badge, rechecked my baggage a second time, and searched my car.

After I was waved through, I finally was allowed to enter the parking lot of the David Skaggs Research Center. Upon entering the building, yet another security officer checked my ID, and called someone to personally escort me into Dr. Bedard's office.

My escort took me down a nondescript hallway, one that might have been in any office building in the world. I met Dr. Bedard just outside his office, where we exchanged pleasantries and a firm handshake. He looked to be in his early- to mid-seventies and stood at about six feet tall. We dropped into comparisons of the weather in our respective towns, but even in this casual bit of chitchat, there was an intensity to his overall demeanor. After our introduction, he showed me into a conference room where, to my complete surprise, a group of scientists, including four Russians, were waiting for me.

★

27

2013

I INTRODUCED MYSELF TO DR. BEDARD'S RUSSIAN colleagues and took a seat. The youngest of the four men, Dr. Valery Zavorotny, who looked to be in his early sixties, admitted he'd stayed up until 2:00 AM the night before, absorbed in Russian websites dedicated to the Dyatlov Pass incident. The others agreed it was indeed a very popular topic of debate in their home country, and they were eager to hear my findings. I told them that I was far more interested in hearing what they and Dr. Bedard had to say.

Nevertheless, I was subjected to a volley of ice-breaking questions: How had I come to be writing about the case? What had I discovered so far? Had I met the Dyatlov group's only survivor? What did he have to say, if anything? And then Zavorotny deadpanned: "Is it true that the only survivor was forced to turn back because of diarrhea?" I laughed, but Zavorotny explained that the belief that indigestion had saved Yudin's life wasn't uncommon in the Russian blogosphere. After I told him that Yudin had, in fact, turned around for far more serious a condition than gastrointestinal distress, Bedard asked some questions of his own, eager to rule out every other viable angle before moving on to a discussion about weather phenomena. I counted off four or five of the most likely theories that had been put forward over the years, and why they could be discounted with near certainty.

Bedard then proposed a theory of his own: Was it possible the hikers had been afflicted with carbon monoxide poisoning? If their tent stove had not been properly ventilated, the resulting toxic air might have resulted in acute disorientation and dizziness. I told them that the hikers had not built a fire that night, nor had they assembled their stove. The Russians then started in with more common questions:

Why didn't the hikers return to their tent? I explained that with the moon not having yet risen, it would have been impossible to see anything, let alone the tent.

Might a bear or wolf have attacked the tent? No. Besides it being illogical for the hikers to flee the protection of their tent at the appearance of a predator, there had been no evidence of animals attacking the tent or the hikers.

What about alcohol? Could the hikers have been drunk? The hikers had not been drinkers, I told them. The group had packed only a limited supply of medicinal alcohol, the contents of which were found upon discovery of the tent. Even if we supposed that the entire group enjoyed getting secretly intoxicated, the autopsies had turned up no trace of alcohol in their blood.

When my hosts had exhausted these possibilities, I explained that this much was certain: Six of the hikers died of hypothermia after hours of exposure to subzero conditions, and the other three of internal hemorrhaging from a tumble into a ravine. What I really wanted to know was: What sent them fleeing from the tent in the first place? Though infrasound intrigued me, I was only just now investigating the idea, and was still struggling to understand it.

The earliest public applications of infrasound, Bedard told me, had been in the early '50s during the Cold War, when the United States began to measure infrasonic waves generated by the nuclear blasts of secret Soviet bomb tests. These measurements—along with spy photographs—helped the United States determine the extent and progress of the Soviet nuclear program. There has only very recently been a resurgence of interest in infrasonic detection and technology—almost as a form of inaudible noise pollution—but the initial interest in its capabilities years ago had to do with nuclear-bomb-testing detection. In 2009, for example, the United States used infrasound to measure a Korean "event" that turned out to be a nuclear rocket test. Bedard explained that the article I had read in *Physics Today* had also generated renewed interest in the topic. The article, he said, "was written exactly to re-create a community for infrasound research. Apparently it worked."

Bedard then told me about a scientific experiment conducted many years ago—an elegant demonstration of infrasound's effects on humans. In 2003, London researchers looking into the symptoms of infrasonic wave exposure hid an "infrasonic cannon" in the back of a concert hall in South London. An audience of 750 people was then asked to sit through four similar contemporary pieces of music while, unbeknownst to them, two of the pieces included waves generated by the infrasonic device. Afterward, they were asked for their reactions to each piece of music. The results: 165 people (22 percent) confessed to body chills and strange feelings of uneasiness, sorrow, nervousness, revulsion and fear during the infrasonic portions; some of the same 22 percent reported accelerated heartbeat or a sudden memory of an emotional loss. Though the effects experienced by these concertgoers were on the milder end of the spectrum, the idea that infrasound was a hidden, silent instrument lurking among a full orchestra, is a fitting metaphor for how the phenomenon presents itself in nature.

Bedard believes that some people are naturally more sensitive to the effects of these infrasonic waves, while others either appear immune or require more intense or prolonged exposure to experience damaging or unpleasant reactions. Over the years, Bedard has received desperate calls from around the world from people reporting a variety of symptoms with no apparent medical or environmental cause. Sometimes these calls come from the same area or city, such as Taos, New Mexico—in what is known as the "Taos Hum." Similarly, the "Windsor Hum" has for years plagued residents of one Canadian border town (on the border of Detroit, Michigan and Windsor, Ontario, across Lake Huron), making a mess of people's sleep schedules, mental health and quality of life. Though the cause has not been determined with any certainty, many believe the machinery at an industrial factory on Jug Island, midway between both Midwest cities, to be the source of the infrasonic waves.

Not everyone affected by the "hum," however, registers it as an aural sensation. "There are hearers and nonhearers," Bedard explained. "To most people it's a throbbing sensation with a constant feeling of anxiety and fear." Although similar "hum" reports have also been noted in Bristol, England and Bondi, Australia, no one, including Bedard, has found the culprit source of what are believed to be "infrasonic waves." Unfortunately, says Bedard, "Most people can't afford to move away from infrasound."

There are some governments that have attempted to harness the ill effects of infrasound for purposes that, on their face, appear to be Orwellian. "The Israelis have used it for crowd control," he explains—the idea being that when exposed to these waves, people want nothing more than to leave the area. The *Toronto Sun* reported an incident from June 6, 2005, in which witnesses described a minute-long blast of sound emanating from a white Israeli military vehicle. Within seconds, protesters began falling to their knees, experiencing symptoms similar to seasickness. An Israeli military source said that such tactics are intended to "disperse crowds with sound pulses that create nausea and dizziness." Infrasound had been used by Nazi Germany to stir up anger and strong emotions in crowds assembled to hear Hitler speak. Hitler had also ordered infrasound experiments to be conducted on prisoners, who were tortured with an experimental weapon that used compressed air to generate high intensities of low-frequency sound waves.

When I suggested that infrasound seemed like the perfect weapon for war, Dr. Bedard responded, "I'm not a believer." In response to a suggestion that Soviets had developed similar weapons during the Cold War, he said, "I wouldn't be surprised if the Russians attempted it, but it would be very difficult to direct infrasound because the wavelengths are so long." I was coming to understand that infrasound as a method of short-range crowd control was feasible, but the existence of long-range infrasound weapons was implausible at best.

Eager to get back to the fate of the Dyatlov hikers, I began to pull out my images of Boot Rock, as well as Russian contour maps of the area surrounding the rock. That's when Bedard asked me if I'd heard of "Kármán vortex street." I had. In fact, the Russian scientist that Borzenkov was in contact with had mentioned Kármán vortex street as a phenomenon that had likely occurred at Boot Rock the night of February 1—though, again, I hadn't fully understood what that meant.

While Bedard and his colleagues pored over the maps and images of Boot Rock, I was given a quick primer on the phenomenon. Kármán vortex street, named after Hungarian physicist Theodore von Kármán, is an occurrence in fluid dynamics of both liquids and gases. In the aerodynamics of weather phenomena, air vortices—or small tornadoes—are created when wind of a certain speed hits a blunt object of a particular shape and size. Geographic masses around the world are known to cause this particular pattern of vortices. When these vortices are large or when revved up at a higher speed, they can reach the destruction threshold of a tornado. For instance, when strong winds hit the Rock of Gibraltar, the powerful vortices spinning off the rock are believed to be the cause of capsized ships in the Strait. These same destructive vortices are oftentimes accompanied by the twin danger of infrasonic frequencies.

Bedard showed me animated models of the pattern, including one of a water tunnel, in which Kármán vortices spun off both sides of an obstructing object. He then played me audio recordings of infrasound from a tornado, which, he explained, had been sped up and played back at 400 hertz to make the infrasound audible. The recording started off as a faint rumbling, then churned into an ominous groan that seemed to expand in decibels like the bellowing foghorn of a ship. In addition to the infrasound waves, these tornadic vortices are also capable of producing audible, ear-splitting groans, often compared to the sound of a freight train.

Bedard and his team continued to study the visuals I had laid out, showing particular interest in two images of Boot Rock. The rock, they pointed out, was irregularly shaped. To create the ideal conditions for Kármán vortex street, the object has to be of a certain symmetry and smoothness. In fact, when new buildings are constructed in windblown areas, they are often designed by architects to be complex in shape in order to dampen the effects of Kármán vortex.

Finally, Bedard looked up at me. He concluded, "Boot Rock would produce a slight roar with different frequencies, but . . ." he shook his head with certainty, "it wouldn't create a Kármán vortex." His colleagues in the room nodded in unified agreement. After fielding a few more questions about how Boot Rock might have generated some other type of infrasound phenomenon, Bedard shook his head again, saying, "Boot Rock is strange, and I'm sure you'd like to blame it, but it's just a pussycat. And it's not producing a harmful Kármán vortex or infrasound."

He turned to the topographical maps again. "Essentially, Boot Rock created a little roar from the high winds but such experienced hikers would not be scared of it. Not to mention, the hikers were over a mile away from Boot Rock, so the sound would have been weak."

I asked if he might be persuaded to look at more pictures of the rock, from different angles. He said he was happy to review whatever

Boot Rock. Photo taken by search party, 1959.

I sent him, but he made it clear that the Boot Rock theory—proposed by myself, Borzenkov and the Russian scientists—was just not likely. And with that verdict, I was transported back to where I had been over a year ago on the mountaintop. With nothing.

I said good-bye to Bedard's Russian colleagues, who wished me well on my quest. Then, with nothing left to discuss, Dr. Bedard offered to show me around the facilities—a guided, personal tour. I followed him down the hall and into his office. Considering that he had managed to destroy all my hopes of potentially solving this case, he seemed lighthearted, even happy to be hosting a tour of his workplace. His office adhered to the controlled chaos that one might expect of a scientist's personal space: There were stacks of drawers with cryptic labels, such as "Glass House" and "Kelly's Eye." On a desk covered in papers sat a can of fog fluid and a miniature elephant supporting a cheerful sign that read: "I love infrasound." I had certainly come to the right place to have the theory of infrasound totally eliminated. Now what?

★

AT THE HOTEL THAT NIGHT, I REVIEWED THE IMAGES I had shown Bedard and his colleagues that day. Not ready to completely discount weather phenomena and infrasound, I had asked Bedard if he could meet with me once more before I returned to Los Angeles. I could not shake the feeling that there was something substantial here. Borzenkov had felt it, too—he had, after all, been my oracle for this entire case—which only made me more reluctant to abandon the idea. I remembered how one of the search volunteers that winter in 1959 had described the hikers' abandonment of their tent as the behavior of "lunatics." Didn't the effects of infrasound produce this same brand of lunacy?

Hoping that Bedard and his colleagues had perhaps misjudged Boot Rock's complex shape and size, I sorted through the folders on my computer and e-mailed the physicist more images of the formation—and from every imaginable angle. I then sent Bedard a quote from the 1959 criminal case, in which an Ivdel local describes the weather of this region: "In winter in the northern Ural Mountains, and even in the summer, there can be strong winds and sometimes whirlwinds. . . . During whirlwinds, various sounds arise in the mountains, terrifying and foreign, like the howls of animals or human moans. . . . You get scared when you are there, and those who haven't heard anything like that can become frightened."

I also sent a few images of the site of the tent, including one particular image of Holatchahl mountain. It gave me chills every time I looked at it. Maybe it was because it reminded me of standing on that same slope, peering through the haze at that eerie, bald summit, devoid of life. Beyond the Holatchahl summit was the peak of Otorten Mountain, the hikers' ultimate destination, which some said translated to: "Don't go there." This, however, is not true. The word Otorten is not a Russian or Mansi word at all, but simply an error on Russian maps resulting from the mispronunciation of a different mountain a few miles to the north. The Mansi actually refer to Otorten by the name Lunt-Husap-Sjahyl, meaning "Mountain of Goose Nests."

I sent Bedard everything I could think of, then closed my laptop and walked to the restaurant downstairs. After devouring a meal of atomic chicken wings, chased back with one too many beers, I returned to my room and promptly fell asleep, hoping the answer would hit me in the shower the following morning.

THE NEXT MORNING, AFTER ANOTHER ROUND OF SECURITY checks, I was back at NOAA. Bedard met me at 10:00 AM in the lobby with a smile on his face, though I couldn't imagine why. As we walked down the hall to his office, he told me he had gotten the photos that I'd sent him. One photo in particular had caught his attention, he said. It reminded him of a weather event in Boulder several years before, in which a nearby elevation, Flagstaff Mountain, had created the conditions for Kármán vortex street, and therefore infrasound. Bedard himself had been there to record a recurrence of the incident, which seemed all the more fantastic for its manifestation in such proximity to the NOAA offices and his place of work.

He then brought me into a conference room, a smaller one than the first. After we sat down, he pulled out a printed photograph of Holatchahl mountain, the one I had sent him the night before.

"It's not because of Boot Rock," he told me, "but because of this dome on the top of the mountain." As he traced the top of the snowy mountain with his finger, he observed, "It's a nice and symmetrical, dome-shaped object."

Hardly believing what he'd just said, I had to ask him to repeat it. The symmetrical dome shape of the summit, he explained, combined with its proximity to the tent's location, would have created the ideal conditions for Kármán vortex. With everything

I had told him about the weather in the area, the lack of anything growing on the top of the mountain, the topographical maps combined with the Ivdel quote from the criminal case, he determined that, "All these descriptions tell me that there are repetitive wind events that happen there."

"Wait," I asked him, "so was it Kármán vortex or infrasound?"

Both, he said. It would be difficult to come up with a more ideal confluence of weather and landscape to create Kármán vortex street—with vortices that would produce infrasound. These vortices would have been screaming right outside the hikers' tent that night, creating an intense discomfort and fear that they couldn't begin to understand. "I can imagine they're all in the tent," Bedard said. "They start to hear the winds pick up. . . . Then to the south they start to feel a vibration in the ground. They hear a roar that seems to pass them from west to east. They start to feel more vibration in the floor, the fabric of the tent vibrates. Another roar of a freight train passes by, this time from the north. . . . The roaring sounds turn horrifying, their chest cavities begin to vibrate from the infrasound created by the stronger vortex now passing. Effects of infrasound are beginning to be felt by the hikers—panic, fear, trouble breathing—as physiological frequencies are generated."

From what Bedard was telling me, it sounded as if the nine hikers, on the night of February 1, 1959, had likely picked the worst spot in that entire area of the northern Ural Mountains to pitch their tent. "I can envision in my mind," he said, "that this would have been a truly frightening scenario . . . for anyone."

Dr. Bedard then summed up my entire three-year quest in a beautifully concise way: "What you're really trying to do is reverse-engineer a tragic event without any witnesses." But without any witnesses, without my having been there on Holatchahl mountain on that night in February, there was no way for me—or anyone—to know with absolute certainty what sent the hikers fleeing from

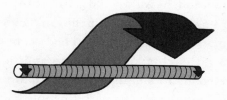

Figure 1: Wind shear is caused by friction with the surface,
increasing with height as it travels up the mountain,
and rolling up to create a horizontal roll vortex or tornado.

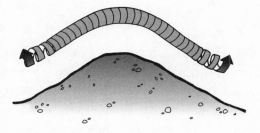

Figure 2: As the horizontal vortex rolls over the dome of
the mountain, it is tilted upward and strengthens into a pair of
vertical tornadoes or vortices.

Figure 3: These vortices pass on both sides of the tent and
continue down the slope until they dissipate.

their tent. Yet at that moment, listening to Dr. Bedard describe how the mountain and the wind could generate this elegant pattern of swirling air—and therefore the panic-inducing infrasound—I found it the most convincing theory I had yet heard.

Besides experiencing an immediate and intense sense of relief, I marveled at the simplicity of it: All along, the culprit had been the mountain that the native people had so ominously named. Had you told me three years ago that the elevation at 1,079 meters, what the Mansi called "Dead Mountain," could have been so directly responsible for the hikers' tragic end, I would never have believed it.

ON FEBRUARY 15, 2013, THE DAY AFTER I RETURNED HOME from Boulder, an infrasound event hit western Siberia. I didn't initially connect the event to infrasound. Like most people who read the news that morning, I registered the occurrence as a gee-whiz oddity—if an alarming one. Just after dawn, at 9:20 local time, a twelve-thousand-ton meteor exploded in the sky over the Ural Mountains, 120 miles south of Yekaterinburg. NASA scientists estimated its diameter to have been 55 feet, making it the largest meteor to hit Earth's atmosphere in over a century since the Tunguska meteor event of 1908. That meteor—thought to have been approximately 130 feet across—had resulted in an explosion that flattened 800 square miles of forest in central Siberia, with a blast several hundred times more powerful than the atomic bomb dropped on Hiroshima.

Unlike the remote Tunguska event, the meteor on February 15 struck the atmosphere above Chelyabinsk, a city of more than one million people. The meteor broke apart between 12 and 15 miles above Earth, in a bright white explosion accompanied by an intense aftershock. The pressure of the explosion blew out windows across Chelyabinsk—a million square feet of glass by one estimate—and injured more than 1,200 people.

Not only one of the largest meteor events in recorded history, the Chelyabinsk meteor was also one of the most documented. Motorists all over the region had recorded the event on their "dash cams"—a popular added feature on Russian cars—with many of those drivers able to view the event from the safe distance of Yekaterinburg, where citizens could see a flaming fireball streaking across the southern sky.

Having been at NOAA just the day before, I shouldn't have been surprised to learn that a by-product of the meteor blast had been infrasound waves, generated when fragments of the rock decelerated in the atmosphere. These subsonic waves had been picked up by a global network of infrasound sensors, operated by the Comprehensive Test Ban Treaty Organization (CTBTO), an international body established for the purposes of monitoring nuclear detonations. On February 15, the CTBTO network measured infrasonic waves as far as Antarctica, more than 9,000 miles from Chelyabinsk. Though the waves were capable of traveling thousands of miles, the effects of the infrasound in Chelyabinsk itself were relatively short-lived. This was not the sustained infrasound as would be generated by a Kármán-vortex-street wind event, but a swift and violent burst of infrasonic waves. According to scientists, the infrasound resulting from the meteor's deceleration had, in part, been responsible for the shattering of windows in Chelyabinsk.

Over the next few days, news of the event included reportage of the infrasound sensor network and numerous mentions of the subsonic waves and their effects—bearing out Dr. Bedard's affirmation that the science of infrasound had been enjoying increased recognition over the past decade. Though monitoring of infrasound had begun years earlier, during the Cold War, the understanding and detection of the phenomenon is not close to what it is today. The first CTBTO global infrasound detector went online in April 2001, followed by more than forty sensors over the next decade. Currently, 45 of the 60 planned sensors of the CTBTO network are up and running.

The more I learned about the increasing sophistication of infrasonic wave detection, the more convinced I became that the connection between infrasound and the fate of the Dyatlov hikers could only have been made fairly recently. As Bedard explained, it has only been in the last decade or so—dating from around the time of Bedard and Georges' 2000 paper in *Physics Today*—that funding for infrasound science, and therefore a clearer understanding of its occurrence in nature, had gained any traction.

Could Lev Ivanov, working as a lead investigator in 1959, have come anywhere near to determining that infrasound had a role in the deaths of nine hikers in the Ural Mountains? Kármán vortex street aside, would Ivanov have known what infrasound was? Likely not. Nevertheless, Ivanov had done all he could with the information available to him at the time. When faced with a baffling set of circumstances that seemed to point to phenomena beyond his understanding, it's not surprising that he would have entertained theories of "orbs" and UFOs.

Some thirty years later, after his retirement, Ivanov put his feelings about the case in writing. With glasnost and perestroika recently enacted, Ivanov was now free to discuss the case publicly. In his letter to the *Leninsky Put* newspaper, Ivanov took the chance to apologize to the hikers' families for the secretive way in which the case had been handled: "I use this article to apologize to the families of the hikers, especially that of Dubinina, Thibault-Brignoles and Zolotaryov. At that time, I tried to do whatever I could, but, as lawyers call it, 'compelling force' was the ruling then and could only be overturned now."

As for what had happened to the hikers, Ivanov alluded to the unknowable: "I had a clear idea of the sequence of their deaths from a thorough examination of their bodies, clothes and other data. Only the sky and its contents—with unknown energy beyond human understanding—were left out."

While Ivanov had lacked the means to accurately explain a nearly incomprehensible event, he had used the resources and vocabulary available to him at the time. Ivanov's written conclusion on May 28, 1959, that the hikers had been the victims of an "unknown compelling force" is one that has come to define the mystery surrounding the case. Though the phrase falls far short of an explanation, the conclusion had been strangely accurate. If infrasound generated by Kármán vortex street had indeed been responsible for the hikers' leaving their tent that night—and, as a result, walking to their deaths—"unknown compelling force" was, at the time, as close as Lev Ivanov—or anyone—could have come to naming the truth.

★

28

The following is a re-creation of February 1, and the early morning hours of February 2, using the hikers' diary entries, weather reports, physical evidence and expert scientific opinion.

FEBRUARY 1–2, 1959

THE FIRST DAY OF FEBRUARY ARRIVES, BRINGING WITH it one of the most carefree mornings of the hikers' trip. The sky is overcast, the wind still, and the hikers linger in their tent over hot cocoa and breakfast. Afterward, pencils and paper come out, and, amid laughter and teasing, the friends draft issue #1 of their mock newspaper, *The Evening Otorten*. The paper is stocked with references and inside jokes accumulated over the course of their trip and years of friendship. When they are finished, an editorial at the top urges: "Let's mark the XXIst session of the Communist Party with increased birth rate of hikers!" In engineering news, a review of a hiking sleigh designed by "Comrade Kolevatov" impishly concludes that while it is "perfect for riding in a train, in a truck and on a horse," it is "not recommended for cargo freight on snow." Above it, the science pages announce: "Scientific society leads vivid discussions about existence of snowman. Latest data show that snowmen dwell at northern Urals, around Otorten Mountain." Whether by "snowmen," the writers meant the abominable kind or a winking reference to themselves, only they could know.

With their high spirits lingering, the friends start to pack up camp, and in the process snap a few playful photographs outside the tent. Once the tent is rolled and stowed away, they begin construction of the *labaz*, the shelter that will hold the supplies for their return trip. There is no sense in hauling nonessentials— extra food, spare skis, boots—up Otorten Mountain. Though Georgy has difficulty parting with his mandolin, he knows that the trade-off of a lighter pack will be worth two days without music. The construction and packing of the *labaz* occupies most of the day, and it's not until midafternoon that the skiers are finally on their way.

As the hikers move away from the protection of the woods, their smiling faces of that morning harden into expressions of sober concentration. The higher they climb, the more challeng-ing the weather becomes, and by midday, their bodies are bowed single-file into the headwind. The photographers among them snap a few images of the group skiing into an ashen haze. With sunset arriving at 5:00 PM, and the storm clearly worsening, it's time to scout a campsite.

Around 4:30 PM, the group pauses in an open area on the east-facing slope of a nameless mountain, known on maps only as "height 1,079" (what will later come to be named Holatchahl). Igor concludes that this is their spot. The slope isn't steep enough for avalanches to be a concern, yet it is above the timberline and exposed to the elements, which is exactly the sort of challenge they are looking for. Ambitious hikers, after all, don't earn the distinc-tion of Grade III by playing it safe in the shelter of the trees. The spot also happens to be in direct sight of their destination, and at sunrise, after a quick breakfast, they will be better suited to quickly packing up and heading straight up Otorten Mountain. They make a note to themselves to photograph the site in the morning, as documentation for the hiking commission.

Setting up camp, of course, takes much longer than it does to dismantle it—a fact that only seasoned outdoorsmen can truly appreciate—and, for the next few hours, the nine hikers work together to erect their canvas fort against the rapidly approaching night. With the wind from the west ever increasing, their efforts take longer than usual—every safeguard must be checked and double-checked to ensure the tent's security on the slope. The team begins by unhooking the skis from their boots and placing eight pairs on the snow, side by side like floorboards. The ninth set of skis they use as vertical support to keep the platform from moving. Someone sticks the ice ax in the snow, keeping it on hand in case they need to use it as a tent support. With the foundation intact, the team begins to unfurl the 6-x-13–foot tarpaulin. The thick material beats vigorously in the wind as they struggle to pull the tent into three dimensions. Finally, with the cords fastened to ski poles planted firmly in the snowpack, the tent is raised vertically where it begins to take on its familiar shape. By the time it is upright, the tent is positioned sideways on the slope, with the entrance facing south.

As is by now routine, Zina and Lyuda are first inside. At 80 square feet, the tent is roomy and tall enough to stand in. By the light of their flashlights, the two begin to fill out the space with the evening's necessities—stove, food, blankets—while arranging the newly emptied backpacks on the floor for insulation. Above the packs, they roll out several blankets. Any unpatched holes in the tent they stuff with clothing or jackets. With the combined efforts both in and outside the tent, the structure is becoming firmly rooted on the slope and insulated from the cold leaking up from below. Not even gale-force winds tear the tent from its spot.

While Sasha and Kolya finish securing the integrity of the tent outside, the other five men—Igor, Doroshenko, Kolevatov, Georgy and Rustik—join the women inside. They help Zina and Lyuda finish arranging the packs and blanket. With that done, the seven of them yank off their damp boots and shed their jackets, spreading them out strategically to dry. This is the group's fifth night of camping, and every boot and jacket has its place.

Outside, the wind is picking up speed, falling somewhere between a whistle and a howl. The half-open entrance flaps urgently. At last, Sasha and Kolya come inside and close up the three layers of toggle clasps, hanging a sheet in front of the entrance for added insulation. By 9:00 PM, the hikers' combined body heat has begun to warm the tent a little. They settle on a light dinner, and ham and biscuits are passed around and eagerly devoured. With their stomachs filling up, some of the hikers have already begun to stretch out, lying on their sides to keep the least amount of surface area from touching the cold ground. Kolya and Sasha, who have arrived late, are still playing catch up with dinner. They continue to wear their outermost layers of clothing and the lining of their boots, perhaps because they will be sleeping on the periphery of the tent. Or perhaps Kolya leaves his boot liners on to excuse himself for a moment; there is no point in bothering with his boots if he's only stepping out to take a leak. Georgy pulls off his watch and hands it to Kolya, who has been tasked with the morning's wake-up call. Kolya has his own watch, but the mechanics of windup watches are known to be unreliable in subzero weather. Better to be safe with a backup watch than to risk sleeping through half the morning.

While some of the hikers continue to snack on cold food, Zina and Doroshenko set the camping stove in the center of the tent. Made of folding cast-iron panels and outfitted with a collapsible chimney that must be twisted into proper shape, the stove is extremely tricky to put together, particularly with cold hands. According to their mock sports page in *The Evening Otorten*, the champion stove assemblers' record is one hour, two minutes and 27.4 seconds. But on that night, the stove just sits there in pieces. Perhaps Zina and

Doroshenko change their minds about assembling it—after all, their route has been taking them ever farther away from the tree line, and they must now conserve wood for their journey up the barren face of Otorten Mountain. Someone dissolves a pack of cocoa in water, but, for lack of a fire, the drink stands cold. Maybe Zina and Doroshenko fail to assemble the stove because something has begun to happen outside, and they are growing increasingly uneasy. The skis beneath the tent have begun to vibrate and the tarpaulin starts to sway.

For the past hour, the wind has been picking up speed as it moves over the dome of the mountain. But most alarming is its volume. The hikers are used to the haunting cry of mountain gales, but the wind's terrifying roar is closer to that of a freight train tearing down the hill past the tent—or rather a series of trains. Igor and his friends know nothing of this weather phenomenon, and when their bodies begin to respond to it, they have no earthly idea what is happening to them. Those who are lying down, sit up in alarm. Their heads begin to pound, as if they've all been struck with the same terrible migraine, and their chests vibrate strangely. This initial feeling of indeterminate anxiety rapidly worsens, until it manifests as full-blown, excruciating terror. By the time the wind outside has reached an infrasonic threshold, the hikers are no longer just anxious about the wind—a deeper fear has set in.

What is happening to us? This may not even be a question they are capable of posing to themselves. The effects of the infrasonic frequencies have temporarily robbed them of their rational minds, and now they are operating under the more primal instinct of flight response. All the hikers want to do is stop the intense discomfort, to get away from it. It's as if the tent is a swiftly sinking ship, and the hikers must abandon it, at all costs, even at the risk of drowning. *Get out, get out, get out,* is all they can think.

Sasha and Kolya undo the latches, just enough to allow them to push themselves out of the flaps at the bottom. Someone at the other end grabs a knife and hacks at the back of the tent, but because the tent's walls are frozen with condensation, the first attempts don't take, and it's only the third stab that successfully tears through the canvas. The opening is just big enough for the hikers to push through, and, one by one, they exit the tent and fly into the darkness. It is twenty-five degrees below zero. The hikers are insufficiently dressed and in their stockinged feet. They are looking only for relief from the torment that has hijacked their bodies; but, in fleeing the tent, they are only escaping from one pain into another.

Though the seven men and two women cannot see it, the wind is tearing off the mountaintop in twin files of vortices. It is, in fact, an army of winter tornadoes, with each rotating column of air hugging the contours of the summit before spinning off on either side of the slope. These vortices barrel past the hikers at 40 mph with an internal wind rotation between 113 and 157 mph, the equivalent of an F2 tornado. The twisters have since grown in size—100 feet wide and 130 feet tall—and in addition to their audible roar, they are generating an infrasonic frequency that has been wreaking havoc on the hikers' minds. But despite the tornadoes' size and power, the hikers are in little danger of being swept away as they flee into the darkness. The tornadoes are swirling past the tent at a substantial distance, giving the hikers a wide berth to clear the tent and descend the slope. Additionally, the farther from the summit the vortices move, and the larger they become, the less powerful their internal spin, and their life-span is no longer than a minute.

The group is separated early. The moon has not yet risen and the night is pitch black. Kolya and Sasha, who were nearest the entrance, have brought their flashlights, but, in the turmoil, Sasha drops his in the snow. The combination of exiting the tent at different times and the complete darkness results in the hikers' dividing into smaller groups. Besides this, they can barely hear each other. In ideal conditions, the sound of their voices would carry a distance of 60 feet, but as they descend the slope with the wind at their backs, the roar around them makes communication nearly impossible.

By the time the hikers have cleared the mountain and are nearing the tree line, the psychotropic effects of the infrasound begin to soften. The pain and confusion has not left their bodies entirely—and the howl of the wind still echoes in their ears—but they are slowly gaining possession of rational thought, and one by one, the nine become overwhelmed by a completely different sort of disorientation. It begins to occur to some of them what they have done, and as the cold pierces their feet, a deep horror sets in. They are standing in subzero conditions, unable to make out a thing in the moonless night, and they have little idea where they are in relation to the tent.

They are, in fact, roughly 300 yards away from the tent, and divided into separate groups of four, three, and two—Lyuda, Kolya, Sasha and Kolevatov; Zina, Rustik and Igor; and Georgy and Doroshenko. The hikers likely realize at this point that fighting the wind all the way back up the slope in hopes of finding the tent in the dark would be impossible. Their only hope is to keep going with the wind at their backs deeper into the trees, and focus on surviving until sunrise. This supposes that, before then, they don't succumb to hypothermia, the symptoms of which have already arrived. Their heart rates are still accelerated from their flight down the slope and from the shock of hitting subzero air, but in the coming hours their heart rates and breathing will slow, and a disorientation that had begun as a response to infrasonic waves will become a delirium brought on by extreme cold.

Georgy and Doroshenko follow a path to the south that leads them across the frozen Lozva River toward the woods. But they encounter deep snow in one of the river's tributaries, and are obstructed from entering into thicker tree cover. So they move along the streambed until they arrive at a large cedar tree. Here, they stop for the night, not knowing just how far they have strayed from the others and from camp. Now begins their difficult task of building a fire, a daunting prospect in total darkness. Doroshenko manages to climb the cedar tree and breaks off small dry twigs for kindling, tossing them down to Georgy. When there are no more twigs, Doroshenko begins to saw at the thicker branches with a pocket knife. But because hypothermia is taking its toll on his coordination, he loses his balance and falls on top of the branches and onto the ground below. He injures himself, and likely gets the wind knocked out of him, but this is nothing compared with the unbearable cold that is paralyzing both men. They are fortunate that cedar is a fairly dry wood, capable of burning in this climate, unlike fir or birch. Additionally, the precaution of sewing matches into their clothing pays off, and with the help of a handkerchief to encourage the flame, the men are able to start a fire with the assembled twigs and branches. The better option would have been to set the entire tree alight, which would likely have provided them with enough warmth for the rest of the night. But they are not thinking properly at this point, and this basic survival tactic doesn't occur to either of them. Instead, they immediately collapse next to their modest fire, letting its warmth—and a strange sense of peace—fall over them.

Meanwhile, Kolya, Lyuda, Sasha and Kolevatov head in the opposite direction, just north of Georgy and Doroshenko. Kolya injures himself at some point, probably on the rocks hiding just inches beneath the snow, causing him to lose his ability to walk. He also loses his flashlight in the process, and now the four must grope blindly through the darkness. Sasha and Kolevatov carry the injured Kolya over the snow in the general direction of the trees, but without warning, they encounter a 24-foot precipice and tumble into the rock-lined ravine below. Kolya, Lyuda and Sasha hit the rocks with massive force—all three sustaining grave chest injuries while Kolya's skull is dashed on the rocks.

Somehow, Kolevatov has managed to avoid seriously injuring himself in the impact—perhaps because Kolya cushioned his fall—and his only concern now is to save the lives of his friends. Perhaps he is able to communicate with them as they are losing consciousness, and in order to keep them warm, he spreads out a bed of fir twigs for them to lie on. He doesn't bother to build a fire, as there is no fuel, and the wood of the surrounding birch and fir trees holds too much moisture to ignite. But, at some point, Kolevatov notices a glow coming from the direction from which they came. The hope of reuniting with the others, and recruiting their help in saving those in the ravine, is the only thing that compels his painfully frozen feet over 450 feet of snow in the direction of the flame.

When he reaches the cedar tree, he finds Georgy and Doroshenko lying unconscious near an already smoldering fire. They were lucky to have started a fire at all, but when one is suffering from severe hypothermia, there is the danger of "afterdrop" upon sudden reintroduction to heat, a phenomenon that, in fact, decreases core body temperature. The sudden warmth from the fire has had a strong soporific effect on the two men, resulting in their slipping into deep unconsciousness. In addition to the fatal mistake of neglecting to keep the fire stoked, the men have let their arms fall into the fire pit in an eagerness to warm themselves. Their clothes and skin are now charred. Kolevatov pulls his friends' limbs from the pit, but it no longer matters: The effects of hypothermia have already killed them. Kolevatov's only thought now is getting back to the ravine to help the three who have fallen. He pulls out his pocketknife and begins to cut away the warmest of Georgy and Doroshenko's clothing—leaving the remaining scraps in shreds. He then moves his friends' bodies side by side, in the most respectful arrangement he can manage, and starts back to the ravine.

By the time he returns, shredded sweaters and pants in his arms, Lyuda, Kolya, and Sasha are just barely alive. He uses part of a sweater to wrap Lyuda's exposed feet, but it is becoming too late to save her. She loses consciousness and will eventually die of her internal injuries. Kolya, who has been knocked unconscious, will succumb to brain hemorrhaging. Only Sasha is still alive, and in a last effort to get him to the protection of the woods, Kolevatov lifts the injured veteran. But Kolevatov is unable to get as far as the edge of the ravine, and, unable to fight the cold and his exhaustion any longer, Kolevatov collapses next to his friend. They both close their eyes, clutching each other as they fall into a peaceful unconsciousness.

Igor, Rustik and Zina have remained closest to the tent, but have become separated from one another. Igor settles into a tree-lined ravine where he suffers the final stages of hypothermia. Even if he had been carrying matches with him, the surrounding birches would have made poor firewood. He is cold and alone, without so much as the company of his friends, who are less than 200 yards away. He collapses next to a small birch, gripping its branches until his final breath. Rustik falls on some stones and fractures his skull. He loses consciousness, but ultimately succumbs to the cold. Zina also injures herself on a stone, breaking her nose. With blood running down her face, she attempts to crawl back up the slope in the direction of the tent, but she loses muscle strength, collapses, and dies of hypothermia.

By the time the waning crescent moon rises at 3:00 AM, radiating blue behind the cloud cover, all nine hikers are motionless. They are frozen in various positions of surrender and intense struggle. In savage winter conditions, and over a vast stretch of ground, all nine fought for their own and one another's lives with the bravery and endurance worthy of Grade III hikers. It was a distinction they would never earn, but one that each of them so rightly deserved.

CAST OF CHARACTERS

THE HIKERS

Yuri Doroshenko "Doroshenko": January 29, 1938–February 1–2, 1959 (21 years old). A student of radio engineering at UPI.

Lyudmila Dubinina "Lyuda": May 12, 1938–February 1–2, 1959 (20 years old). The youngest of the Dyatlov group, and one of two women. A student in the construction school at UPI, with an emphasis on economics.

Igor Dyatlov "Igor": January 13, 1936–February 1–2, 1959 (23 years old). The leader of the Dyatlov hiking group—a radio enthusiast, photographer and engineering student at UPI.

Alexander Kolevatov "Kolevatov": October 16, 1934–February 1–2, 1959 (24 years old). A student of nuclear physics at UPI.

Zinaida Kolmogorova "Zina": January 12, 1937–February 1–2, 1959 (22 years old). One of two women in the Dyatlov hiking group. A student of radio engineering at UPI.

Yuri Krivonishchenko "Georgy": February 7, 1935–February 1–2, 1959 (23 years old). A student of construction and hydraulics at UPI.

Rustem Slobodin "Rustik": January 11, 1936–February 1–2, 1959 (23 years old). Graduated from UPI with a mechanical engineering degree.

Nikolay Thibault-Brignoles "Kolya": June 5, 1935–February 1–2, 1959 (23 years old). Graduated from UPI with a civil construction degree.

Yuri Yudin "Yudin": July 19, 1937–April 27, 2013 (21 years old at time of the incident). The tenth member of the Dyatlov hiking group, who turned back in 1959 because of his chronic rheumatism.

Alexander Zolotaryov "Sasha": February 2, 1921–February 1–2, 1959 (37 or 38 years old). The oldest member of the Dyatlov group. A hiking instructor and a WWII veteran, he worked in a mining factory but was studying to be a military engineer when he joined the hiking group in 1959.

FRIENDS AND FAMILY OF THE HIKERS

Rufina Dyatlova: Igor Dyatlov's younger sister. Like her brother, she was a student in radio engineering at UPI. She was twenty-one at the time of the incident.

Slava Dyatlov: Igor's older brother. His love of hiking and the outdoors inspired Igor to follow his lead. Slava had since graduated from UPI with a degree in radio engineering by the time of the incident.

Tatiana Dyatlova: Igor Dyatlov's younger sister. She was twelve at the time of the incident. Graduated from UPI with a chemical engineering degree.

Stanislav Velikyavichus: A Lithuanian freelance worker and former prisoner who escorted the Dyatlov group to the abandoned geological settlement. The hikers called him "Grandpa Slava."

Yevgeny Venediktov "Boroda" (or "Beard"): A member of the Sector 41 woodcutter settlement.

THE 1959 INVESTIGATIVE AND SEARCH TEAMS

Georgy Atmanaki: A search and rescue volunteer and a member of the hiking party (along with Shavkunov and Karelin) who witnessed the light orbs in February 1959.

Yuri Blinov: A UPI student, hiking-club member and friend of the Dyatlov group. He was among the first to search for the hikers. Blinov's own hiking group had shadowed Dyatlov's for the first portion of their trip. He was among the last to see the group alive.

Vadim Brusnitsyn: A search volunteer and UPI student who was part of Mikhail Sharavin and Boris Slobtsov's larger search team. His testimony during the investigation helped establish Sharavin and Slobtsov's discovery of the tent.

Lev Gordo: The then-47-year-old director of the UPI sports club. Along with Yuri Blinov, Gordo was among the first to search for the hikers.

Lev Ivanov: Criminal investigator at the Sverdlovsk regional prosecutor's office. He replaced Vasily Tempalov as lead investigator on the Dyatlov case.

Vladislav Karelin: A search volunteer and a member of the hiking party (along with Shavkunov and Atmanaki) who witnessed the light orbs in February 1959.

Abram Kikoin: Brother of famous nuclear physicist Isaak Kikoin. He taught physics at UPI and headed the school's mountaineering club; for that reason, he was assigned to head up a relief search team to look for the missing hikers.

Ivan Laptev: Forensic expert who autopsied the Dyatlov hikers' bodies.

Levashov: Sverdlovsk's chief municipal radiologist, who performed radiation tests on the hikers' clothing and organs at Ivanov's request.

Yevgeny Maslennikov: One of the most experienced outdoorsmen in Sverdlovsk at the time of the hikers' deaths. He had been an adviser to the Dyatlov group and was eventually asked to lead a search party.

Nikolay Moiseyev: A police lieutenant who, with his trained dogs, was among those who found the hikers' bodies.

Colonel George Ortyukov: A lecturer of reserve-officer training at UPI. Heavily involved in the search efforts, he was the first to assemble a formal search party.

Mikhail Sharavin: UPI student and search volunteer. Discovered the hikers' tent with Boris Slobtsov.

Vladimir Shavkunov: a member of the hiking party (along with Karelin and Atmanaki) who witnessed the light orbs in February 1959.

Boris Slobtsov: A UPI student, search volunteer and a friend of the Dyatlov hikers. Slobtsov discovered the tent along with Mikhail Sharavin.

Vasily Tempalov: The original prosecutor assigned to investigate the case. A junior counselor of justice at the Ivdel prosecutor's office, he was quickly replaced by Lev Ivanov, who outranked him.

Aleksey Vozrozhdyonny: Forensics expert. Conducted the autopsies of the Dyatlov group together with Ivan Laptev.

THE PRESENT-DAY TEAM

Vladimir Borzenkov: A disaster expert, aviation engineer, investigator and leading authority on the Dyatlov case.

Donnie Eichar: Filmmaker, author.

Olga Kuntsevich: Yuri Kuntsevich's wife, resident of Yekaterinburg.

Yuri Kuntsevich: President of the Dyatlov Foundation, hiker and Young Pioneer instructor in Yekaterinburg.

Jason Thompson: Author's producing partner and friend, accompanied him on his first trip to Russia.

Dmitri Voroshchuk: Geologist and translator who participated in the expedition to Dyatlov Pass with the author, Borzenkov and Kuntsevich.

THE HIKERS' TIMELINE

January 23, 1959
The Dyatlov group boards a train in the city of Sverdlovsk and departs to Serov at 9:05 PM.

January 24, 1959
The hikers arrive in the town of Serov at 7:39 AM. They spend the afternoon entertaining children at School #41. In the evening the hikers depart on the train for Ivdel. They arrive in Ivdel around midnight.

January 25, 1959
The hikers board a 6:00 AM bus to Vizhay. Arriving at around 2:00 PM, they are given luxurious accommodations by the director of the free workers' camp.

January 26, 1959
While waiting for their next means of transportation, the hikers seek advice from the town's forester. The hikers then travel by truck to a remote woodcutting settlement in Sector 41 and arrive at 4:30 PM. The hikers spend the night in the workers' dormitory, singing songs and reciting poetry until early the next morning.

January 27, 1959
They wait until for 4:00 PM for a man with a horse and cart to take them to another northern settlement, an abandoned geological site. The hikers travel late into the night up the frozen Lozva River on their way to the site.

January 28, 1959

After a difficult trek up the frozen Lovza River, the Dyatlov hikers arrive in good spirits at the abandoned geological site in the dark early morning hours. The hikers find an empty house and sleep until daylight. Later that day, Yuri Yudin says his final farewell to his friends and returns back home due to poor health. The rest of the group continues skiing north along the Lozva River.

January 29, 1959

The Dyatlov hikers trek further along the Lozva River and set up camp near the frozen Auspiya River.

January 30, 1959

The hikers continue along the Auspiya River and note in their journals the Mansi symbols on the trees. Deep snow begins to make skiing more difficult.

January 31, 1959

The hikers continue upstream on the Auspiya River and set up camp for the night.

February 1, 1959

In the first half of the day, the hikers construct a temporary storage shelter and leave some supplies inside to lighten their packs for the trip up Otorten Mountain. The group then skis all afternoon, arriving at what would become known as Dyatlov Pass at 3:00 PM. The sun sets at 4:58 PM. They set the tent on the eastern slope of Holatchal mountain at an altitude of 1,079 meters (3,540 feet).

THE INVESTIGATION TIMELINE

February 2, 1959
The tenth hiker, Yuri Yudin, returns home to Emelyashevka.

February 12, 1959
The Dyatlov hikers are expected to return to Vizhay. Yudin, who is still in Emelyashevka, forgets to relay the message to Sverdlovsk that the Dyatlov group will be three days late.

February 15, 1959
Relatives of the hikers are unaware of their expected delay and begin to worry when their loved ones fail to return to Sverdlovsk as planned by February 13.

February 16, 1959
Igor's sister, Rufina, alerts school administrators that her brother and the rest of the hiking group have not returned home.

February 17, 1959
Between 6:00–7:00 AM, various hikers, hunters and military personnel in the Ural region report seeing light orbs in the sky.

Bowing to pressure from friends and family of the hikers, university officials send an inquiring telegram to Vizhay, the city from which the Dyatlov group would be traveling.

February 18, 1959

A request for a search plane by the families of the Dyatlov hikers is refused by university administrators.

February 19, 1959

A telegram from Vizhay informs university administrators in Sverdlovsk that the Dyatlov group has not arrived.

Colonel Georgy Ortyukov at UPI begins assembling a formal search party to look for the missing hikers. Yuri Blinov, a UPI student whose group had traveled with Dyatlov's on their first leg of the trip, is among the first to join.

February 20, 1959

A formal search for the nine missing hikers begins. Yuri Blinov and Lev Gordo, president of the sports club of the Ural Polytechnic Institute, fly by helicopter to Ivdel. From Ivdel they take a Yak-12 surveillance plane north to scan the Ural ridge for the missing hikers, but must turn back early due to bad weather.

Yuri Yudin returns to Sverdlovsk from his hometown of Emelyashevka and is informed that his friends have not yet returned.

The Ivdel prosecutor's office orders a criminal investigation into the case of the missing hikers.

February 21, 1959

Vasily Tempalov, an Ivdel prosecutor, is assigned to head the investigation.

Blinov and Gordo fly to the Mansi village of Bahtiyarova to extract what information they can from the local tribe. They learn that a group of young hikers stopped for tea in the village earlier that month.

February 22, 1959

A search party under the leadership of UPI student Boris Slobtsov heads to Ivdel by plane.

February 23, 1959

The search parties arrive by helicopter on the eastern slope of Otorten Mountain, the hikers' intended destination.

Two planes survey the mountain area to the east from Otorten Mountain and the Lozva River banks.

February 24, 1959

Boris Slobtsov's search party surveys the Lozva valley and the Auspiya River. Mountaineering expert Yevgeny Maslennikov arrives from Sverdlosk to join the search. There is an escalation in the search efforts as UPI students, family members, local officials and volunteers from surrounding work camps target various routes to Otorten Mountain.

February 25, 1959

A search helicopter over the Auspiya River picks up ski tracks. Leaflets are dropped from the search plane that instruct Boris Slobtsov's party to alter its route and follow the recently spotted tracks.

February 26, 1959

Searchers Boris Slobtsov and Michael Sharavin discover the Dyatlov hikers' tent at an elevation on the east slope of Holatchahl mountain.

After Slobtsov and Sharavin return to camp, radiogram operator Igor Nevolin sends news to Ivdel that the tent has been found.

February 27, 1959

Search groups converge on Holatchahl mountain. Twenty yards below the tent, nine sets of footprints are found leading from the tent toward the valley.

The bodies of Yuri Doroshenko and Yuri Krivonishchenko are found by a cedar tree a mile downslope from the tent.

The bodies of Igor Dyatlov and Zinaida Kolmogorova are found later that day. Dyatlov is found roughly 1,300 yards from the tent and Kolmogorova about 300 yards from Dyatlov.

February 28, 1959

The search for the remaining hikers continues with no results.

March 1, 1959

Regional criminal investigator Lev Ivanov replaces Tempalov as chief investigator. Ivanov arrives on the scene to begin his investigation of the locations where the bodies were discovered. Ivanov examines the Dyatlov tent site and determines the tent was erected as per hiking regulations.

The first four bodies from the Dyatlov hiking group are taken to Boot Rock and prepared to be flown to Ivdel.

March 2, 1959

The hikers' storage structure is discovered with food rations and personal items belonging to the hikers.

Ivanov and the bodies of the hikers are flown to Ivdel by helicopter.

March 3, 1959

The search for the remaining hikers continues with no results.

March 4, 1959

Forensic examinations of Igor, Zina, Georgy and Yuri begin in Ivdel.

March 5, 1959

Rustem Slobodin's body is found under a foot of snow in the 300-yard distance between Igor Dyatlov and Zinaida Kolmogorova.

March 6, 1959

Rustem's body and the tent's contents are taken to Ivdel by helicopter.

March 7, 1959

Yuri Yudin travels to Ivdel by helicopter to identify the belongings of the Dyatlov group.

March 8, 1959

Yuri Yudin identifies the equipment and personal belongings of the Dyatlov hikers in Ivdel.

March 9–10, 1959

Funerals are held for the first five hikers in Sverdlovsk. Yudin is still in Ivdel and not able to attend the funeral.

March 11, 1959

Forensic examination of Rustem begins in Ivdel as search efforts continue in the Urals.

March 12–16, 1959

Four hikers remain missing: Lyuda Dubinina, Sasha Zolotaryov, Alexander Kolevatov and Kolya Thibault-Brignoles. The search continues.

March 17, 1959
Meteorologists and soldiers in Ivdel report seeing light orbs. A similar phenomenon is observed by search party member Vladislav Karelin as his team was traveling in the northern Urals.

March 18–30, 1959
Forensic examination of Igor, Zina, Georgy, Doroshenko and Rustik conclude that the five hikers had died from hypothermia. The question remains not how they died but under what circumstances.

Search efforts expand to a larger area with no results.

March 31, 1959
Search party members on the Auspiya River report seeing light orbs in the sky of a similar nature to those seen on February 17.

April 1–2, 1959
Harsh weather slows the search effort for the hikers.

April 3–6, 1959
The hikers' tent is examined at Sverdlovsk criminal research laboratory. It's established that the tent was cut by someone and the Dyatlov group escaped suddenly. Ivanov believes the issue of the tent being cut is crucial to solving the case.

April 7–May 2, 1959
A professional tailor examines the slashes in the tent and confirms what investigators have already concluded: It is a deliberate slash made with a knife.

Criminal expert G. Churkina later examines the tears in the tent under a microscope and determines the slashes were made from the inside of the tent, not the outside, by a blade or knife. Ivanov no longer considers the theory of an outside attacker.

Search efforts continue as the teams battle with strong winds and deep snow.

May 3, 1959
Mansi searcher Stepan Kurikov discovers loose branches, cut by a knife, under snow in a ravine near a cedar tree. Probing of the area begins and a piece of clothing is discovered. The team digs a large hole above the creek bed and discovers a cache of cut and shredded clothing.

May 4, 1959
Excavation through snow and slush above the creek bed reveals the remaining four hikers (Lyudmila Dubinina, Alexander Zolotaryov, Alexander Kolevatov and Nikolay Thibault-Brignoles) at the bottom of a ravine. The volunteers remove the badly decomposed bodies from the slush in the ravine.

May 5–6, 1959
Ivanov arrives to examine the condition of the bodies pulled from the ravine.

May 7, 1959
Helicopter pilot, Captain Gatezhenko, refuses to transport the hikers' bodies to Ivdel without zinc-lined coffins to prevent toxic or biological leakage.

May 8, 1959
The remaining four hikers are flown to Ivdel by helicopter in the specified zinc-coated coffins.

May 9, 1959

A forensic examination of the remaining four hikers reveals "violent" injuries to three of the bodies.

May 10–17, 1959

Ivanov interviews more witnesses in an attempt to make sense of the recent autopsy results.

May 18–21, 1959

Ivanov orders radiological analysis for possible radiation contamination.

May 19–21, 1959

Radiological tests are performed on the hikers' organs and clothing samples.

May 22, 1959

Dubinina, Zolotaryov, Kolevatov and Thibault-Brignoles' closed-casket funerals are held for family only.

May 28, 1959

The criminal case is discontinued with Lev Ivanov's conclusion that "an unknown compelling force should be considered the cause of the hikers' deaths."

May 29, 1959

Radiological analysis report comes back after the case has been closed. The radiologist determines articles of the hikers' clothing to contain higher-than-normal levels of radiation.

ACKNOWLEDGMENTS

Many relatives of the hikers, search participants and key people involved in the Dyatlov case have died without knowing what happened to their friends and loved ones. The spirit of this book is in honor of the nine hikers who died, their family and friends.

This book would have been impossible without the assistance of a great number of people.

Without the wisdom, tireless guidance and enduring friendship of Yuri Kuntsevich, Vladimir Borzenkov and Yuri Yudin this book would not exist. I would like to pay special tribute to Yuri Yudin, who passed away before the publication of the book. I hope I've made you proud in retelling your story. Rest in peace my friend.

Dmitriy Voroshchuk for accompanying me on the expedition to the Dyatlov Pass. Tatania Dyatlov and family, Piotr Bartolomey, Evgeniy Zinoviyev, Mikhail Sharavin, Vladislav Karelin, Oleg Arkhipov, Aleksey Budrin, Anatoliy Gushchin, Alexsandra Ivanov, Igor Dubinina, Yuri Koptelov, Aleksey Kashin, Sergey Lugovtsov, Sergey Zuberev, Mikhail Terekhanov, Valeriya Gamatina, Nikolay Roman, Stephan Anyamov, Valentin Yakimenko, Evgeniy Koshkarev, Leonid Rokotyan and Milana Borisova for providing essential recollections from interviews. Katya Bushkovskaya, Olga Taranenko and Eugene Alpirn for providing translations. Lev Ivanov for providing the clues contained in your 1959 case investigation. Many thanks to Olga Kuntsevich for taking me in as family into your home. You are a treasure.

To J.C. Gabel and Nova Jacobs. Without your tireless editing, writing and research contributions, the book would not have been possible.

Steve Mockus, my editor at Chronicle Books, for his superb instinct for narrative and for giving me the space to figure out how to tell this story. Emily Dubin for helping visually frame a difficult and complicated story. Beth Steiner, Lia Brown and Courtney Drew at Chronicle for your help.

The wisdom of experts and scholars: Dr. Al Bedard and Valerie Zavorotney at NOAA Earth System Research Laboratory; Dr. Chris Straus, associate professor of radiology at the University of Chicago Medical Center; Dr.

Yuri Yudin and
Donnie Eichar,
February 2012

Reed Brozen, medical director at Dartmouth–Hitchcock Medical Center's Advance Response Team; Bruce Tremper, director of forest services at the Utah Avalanche Center; Peter Sherwood, professor of Hungarian Language and Culture at the University of North Carolina at Chapel Hill; Russian scholars Jonathan Brent and J. Archibald Getty.

Carolyn Kellogg at the *L.A. Times* for tipping J.C. and me off to Richard Lloyd Parry's brilliant book, *People Who Eat Darkness*, which served as an inspiration for *Dead Mountain*. Paul and Tinti Norton for their friendship, publishing expertise and guidance. Nina Weiner for introducing J.C. and me in the summer of 2011. John Sinclair, Konrad Ribero, Tony Macaluso, Jeremy Rabb, George Hodak, Sybil Perez and Rachel Wiseman, who all read the manuscript with great care. Josh Rogers for hosting a one-night-only salon to help garner additional support for the book.

To my good friend Jason Thompson, thanks for believing when the times were tough.

To my mom and dad for instilling courage in me at a young age, and giving me guidance when I was lost.

And finally to my girlfriend Julia for your shining integrity, your endless optimism and your creative instincts. And to our son Dash and his happy feet. Your smile brings tears to my eyes. You are my inspiration. This book is dedicated to you both.

INDEX